East Meets West in Children's Literature

Pied Piper Publishing

First published 2005 by:

Pied Piper Publishing Ltd.
80 Birmingham Road
Shenstone
Lichfield
Staffordshire
WS14 0JU
www.piedpiperpublishing.com

British Library Cataloguing in Publication
A catalogue record for this book is available from the British Library.

ISBN 0 9546384 6 8

Contents

Preface

East Meets West in Children's Literature: The Context

Pat Pinsent

The eleventh annual conference of the British Section of the International Board on Books for Young People took place at Froebel College, University of Roehampton, in November 2004, and was, as usual well attended. The theme of 'East meets West in Children's Literature' was combined with a celebration of the seventieth birthday of one of the most notable contemporary British writers for children, Diana Wynne Jones, whose fantasies, without being set in a specific 'real' location, are often characterised by the kind of strangeness which was felt by early western explorers of eastern lands. The papers which form the main body of this book were in most instances presented at the conference, but inevitably, some of the plenary speakers and workshop presenters were unable to let us have their papers for this present collection, so below is a summary of these, based in most instances on synopses provided by the speakers themselves. Material related specifically to Diana Wynne Jones is summarised later in this volume.[1]

The first speaker was Uli Knoepflmacher, Paton Professor of Ancient and Modern Literature at Princeton University, who examined 'Victorian and Edwardian figurations of English boys and girls' in the work of Kipling, Ewing, and Burnett. He began however by looking at Mary Norton's 1952 fantasy, *The Borrowers,* in which the significance of literacy is emphasised by the fact that when the unnamed boy character first meets the Lilliputian Arrietty, he promptly asks her whether she can read. Knoepflmacher claimed that this exchange calls attention to the insecurities of a boy whose imperiled imperial identity makes him as much a 'vestigial figure' as the diminishing race of Borrowers who can no longer live off the productions of the 'vast multitudes who outnumber them.' The boy's immersion in an oral culture that relied on a rich mixture of Indian dialects may have retarded his development as a reader of English texts, but it has also allowed him to resist the limitations of 'the print culture his sisters have accepted'.

Thus, whereas both the boy and Arrietty seem to regard bilingualism as a handicap, Mary Norton and Mrs. May (the book's narrator) seem to suggest that the boy's retardation is a decided asset. Indeed, his ability to 'see' tiny beings (which he may have invented to impress his sisters) can actually be read, as Mrs. May slyly implies, as a tribute to the Indian nourishment of his English imagination.

The earlier writers, Rudyard Kipling, Juliana Horatia Ewing, and Frances Hodgson Burnett, all from a period when Victorian folklorists and ethnographers were busily tracing Western fairy tales to their Far Eastern sources, all depict child-protagonists who, like the ten-year-old boy in *The Borrowers,* must shed their regressive attachment to a lost 'aural paradise.' Knoepflmacher claimed that Kipling was much influenced by Ewing's *Six to Sixteen*, which he read at the age of seven, after his painful exile drove him to replace his ayah's oral tales with the 'priceless volumes' his parents sent him from India. It was a book the seventy-year-old Kipling still claimed to know 'almost by heart.' Knoepflmacher suggested that much that Kipling and Burnett were to reprocess in their stories of Anglo-Indian children such as Punch and Kim or Sara Crewe and Mary Lennox is already embedded in the first-person narrative told by Ewing's Margaret Vandalour.

He concluded by suggesting that in *The Borrowers* India persistently operates as an emblem for a 'universal traffic between opposites, between generational, sexual, and cultural binaries that would seem insurmountable - child and adult, girl and boy, native and foreign - and yet continued to tease the rich "bilingual imagination" of the writers who dramatized their conflict'.

Author and TV executive, Farrukh Dhondy, whose work for young adults includes *East End at Your Feet* (1976) and *Come to Mecca* (1978), gave a lively account of his writing career. His contention that the two most important multi-cultural books in English are Mark Twain's *Huckleberry Finn* and Rudyard Kipling's *Kim* challenged his audience; he claimed that the picaresque nature of both of these classics enabled their authors to explore the question 'What is America [or India] about?' Dhondy's own recent *Run* (2002) takes a similar picaresque format, moving through modern Britain. He asserted that too much Indian literature today, for instance, was addressing itself to the West rather than confronting major issues. Where are the modern writers who, like Dostoyevsky in his world, attempt to explain why society is producing disaffected youths who want to blow up society itself? Novels which deal with the conflict in values that exists in the modern world are much needed.

The next plenary session involved a panel of three authors. Tony Bradman gave an account of his compilation of a recent anthology of stories about racism, *Skin Deep: Stories that Cut to the Bone* (Puffin, 2004). He put this together in order to tackle the subject head on, believing fiction to be a very effective way of helping readers to understand why racism happens and what it does to people. Bali Rai, best known for his first novel, *(un)arranged marriage* (Corgi, 2001), discussed the difficulty felt by some British people of Asian background in being sure about their own cultural identity. He admitted his own concern about racist attitudes, including those felt within the Asian community itself. Tanuja Desai Hidier spoke about her novel *Born Confused* (Scholastic, 2003), which has won a range of awards. Without being an autobiography, it does explore some of the key ideas that she developed from her years in New York City, where she came into contact with a thriving

South Asian community, quite unlike the relatively small numbers in Wilbraham, Massachusetts, where she grew up. Two themes she emphasises in her book are the nature of family, whether that of birth or that of choice, and the power of music to make people come together.

Bali Rai also shared a workshop presentation with Rehana Ahmed, researcher and children's fiction editor, who spoke about her anthology of new short stories for teenage readers by South Asian writers based in Britain, *Walking a Tightrope* (Young Picador, May 2004). Bali Rai contributed a story, 'Beaten', to this collection, and the other contributors were Rukhsana Ahmad, Debjani Chatterjee, Farrukh Dhondy, Jamila Gavin, Romesh Gunesekera, Aamer Hussein, Preethi Nair, Shyama Perera and Adam Zameenzad. Focusing on the anthology, and 'Beaten' in particular, Rai and Ahmed debated the politics of representing 'Asian Britain' for a teenage readership, concentrating on questions such as the extent to which negative aspects of racism should be confronted, given the risk of stereotyping and consequently manipulation into a racist, 'them-and-us' discourse. Should Asian writers avoid speaking out about structures of oppression that might be operating within sectors of the Asian community, even if a consequence might be that the stories were used as 'proof' of the stereotypes that circulate about the Asian community? Ahmed says:

> While keen to avoid the role of prescriptive editor, and to enable a diversity of representations which might destabilise a construction of 'Asian Britain' as a homogeneous collective, I also felt it necessary that the anthology should counter the hegemonic 'script' that is written for Asians in Britain by the media and at the level of the state. In the case of 'Beaten', situated in a Sikh Punjabi community in the Midlands, these aims came into conflict where I felt aspects of the story seemed tacitly to endorse stereotypes of 'British Asian' identities, such as the abusive patriarch or the passive female victim of abuse.

She argued that the minority artists' 'burden of representation' is imposed not (or not only) by policing tendencies within their own community but first and foremost by negative hegemonic discourses that reduce Asian (particularly Muslim Asian) culture to a series of damaging clichés which must be challenged. Also important, she felt, was a challenge to the hegemony of the acceptable, consumable face of 'Asian Britain,' mapped out by the media through the exclusion of those elements of difference that cannot be comfortably incorporated into normative British culture and institutions. Her aim that the anthology should diverge from legitimised representations of 'Asian chic' was in tension with an awareness that its effective dissemination would to an extent depend on such representations.

Sandra Williams, Senior Lecturer at the University of Brighton, described her research into children's literature in Singapore, which has resulted in the publication by the National Book Development Council, Singapore, of the first annotated bibliography of children's books in English since independence in I965. She contextualised the development of a distinct Singaporean literature for children, in a country whose multi-cultural population of four million includes Chinese, Malays, Indians and Eurasians. English, used in school instruction and in government, is a unifying language, and children's literature from English speaking countries is readily available in Singapore bookshops and libraries. She went on to discuss the challenges of developing a distinct children's literature in Singapore, which include the difficulty in finding a distinct voice in the colonial language and in building confidence in local literature; being serious about Children's Literature in a society which tends to regard the Arts in general as less significant than industry; and dealing with the challenge of depicting a multi-cultural society. This literature includes folk tales from both Singapore and S.E. Asia; reading scheme books, few of which have a distinct Singaporean setting; and some commercial titles which reflect the Singapore landscape. The construction of a distinct National Identity is a concern for Government and there is much focus on this through the large celebrations on National Day, but currently children's literature is not a major site for such a construction. There appears to be little concern that children are more likely to read 'the other' than themselves. The annotated bibliography may well serve to raise interest in what has been written and give more focus to local books, so that Singapore children can read more about their own lives, culture and landscape.

Gita Wolf, of Tara Publishing, India, felt that her perspective on multicultural literature was likely to be different from that of the other participants of this conference. While most children in the UK are unlikely to have much knowledge about India, those of Indian origin may have a special relationship to the place, sometimes evoked in their homes through nostalgic tales or exotic customs which mean that it is seen as a distant, perhaps idealised, point of reference. Books from India have a place, not so much to supply more authentic information than books from elsewhere, but rather as a way of contributing in a unique way to the field of multiculturalism and its dialogue with questions of identity. This relates to point of view - the way in which a reader (almost unconsciously) accepts the centre from which a book is written. The books she publishes are written from a position that takes itself for granted, and this simple shift in who is telling the tale, and about whom, can be far more radical in its effects than most conscious pedagogy. She illustrated this by a reference to the way in which Indian children grew up with the English school story, dreaming of scones and suspecting 'darkies' as if it was the most natural thing in the world. We forgot for the moment that we, in fact, were 'darkies'. The point is that the converse works just as well: a good book from India, which children in the UK find as exciting as anything else they know, can achieve an unselfconscious shift in their perspective just as easily and playfully. This is a function of all good literature - it communicates effortlessly. Enforced political correctness is much harder going.

The books she presents are based on this premise: to change perspectives, it is vital to bring in many new ones. They are rooted in the Indian context but not exotic; they are for the enjoyment of children everywhere. She sees multiculturalism as the act of bringing in different voices into a homogenized world - not a niche, but a vital part of world children's literature.

The workshop presented by Lisa Sainsbury, Senior Lecturer in English at the National Centre for Research in Children's Literature at the University of Roehampton, introduced Japan's Studio Ghibli. Since it included discussion of the forthcoming adaptation of a novel by Diana Wynne Jones, *Howl's Moving Castle* (1986), it also served as something of a bridge to the concluding section of the conference, details of which will be found later in this volume.

Hayao Miyazaki, the co-founder of Studio Ghibli, has either worked on or directed some of the most influential animated films in Japan, and his work displays the influences of European culture. European influence is to be detected in some of his early *anime* (the Japanese term for 'animated film'). While an undergraduate in the 1960s, Miyazaki joined the children's literature research society and explored a wide range of European children's books. In *Hayou Miyazaki: Master of Japanese Animation* (Berkeley, 2002), Helen McCarthy reveals: 'The young Miyazaki was exposed to a wide range of storytellers who used fantasy and legend in different ways. British writers like Rosemary Sutcliff, Phillipa Pearce, and Eleanor Farjeon, and Europeans such as Antoine de Saint-Exupery, played their part in forming his views of storytelling and character development' (p30). He was one of the first Japanese animators to travel to Europe for artistic inspiration, and his choices of locations suggest an interest in a cultural fusion of East and West. The early *anime* he was involved with reveal numerous references to European Literature: *Gulliver's Space Travels* (1964); *The Little Norse Prince* (1968); *Puss in Boots* (1969); *Moomins* (1970); *Animal Treasure Island* (1971); *Pippi Longstocking* (1971, a project eventually abandoned); *Alpine Girl Heidi* (1974); *Anne of Green Gables* (1979); *Great Detective Holmes* (1984).

Some of the key themes at work in Miyazaki's anime are the detailed landscapes which are often breathtaking (the slowing down to take in scenery really distinguishes Japanese anime from Western animation); a political concern for the environment, sometimes a little heavy-handed; a concern about the use to which technology is put (in *Castle in the Sky* (1986), for example, he approves technology for benevolent purposes but shows how it can be destructive if used for power); the potential for the spiritual or magical in everyday life, frequently attributed to childhood and early adolescence or to artists with spiritual/magical powers – and a depth in time through the operation of legend. Flight is sometimes seen as a special gift of the central characters, while childhood is explored from a range of perspectives, particularly in relation to rites of passage to adulthood, often figured in terms of fantasy. Miyazaki tends to represent the elderly as endowed with wisdom and having a positive relationships with the young; in *Castle in the Sky,* Ma Dola, the Pirate Mother, is given the role of wise observer, despite her moral ambiguity. He presents a large number of strong female leads, and displays an interest in exploring girlhood and the passage into maturity for women, which means that the nature of femininity is explored on several levels. However, the promise of love and/or marriage provides closure in many of his films, sometimes undermining the feminist drive operating in his work. Conflict, and the proximity between life and death, are explored in various ways, and several of his heroines look for alternatives to violence and war. His films are very playful, as he refers self-reflexively to his own work and to a wide range of cultural sources.

This workshop involved the screening of scenes from a selection of Miyazaki's films. It closed with a speculative consideration of the forthcoming *Howl's Moving Castle*. Jones' original book provides the opportunity for Miyazaki to develop many of the themes that interest him. For example, part of the story is set in Wales, a landscape that Miyazaki represented in his depiction of the mining community in *Castle in the Sky*. There is also the potential to explore relationships between the young and old in the transformation of a character from young girl to old woman. Interestingly, an interview with Diana Wynne Jones[2] reveals her admiration for Miyazaki's work, particularly his use of beautiful backgrounds and landscapes.

Notes

1. Fuller versions of these summaries appear in the spring issue of *IBBYLink*, the journal of the British section of IBBY.

2. Nausicaa Website: translation of interview with Diana Wynne Jones from the *Yomiuri* Newspaper, http://www.nausicaa.net/miyazaki/howl/impressions.html (accessed 7.11.04)

Introduction

East Meets West in Children's Literature

Pat Pinsent

A major source of strife in the world today is that which derives from the inability and unwillingness of different cultural groups to be open to learning, on anything other than a superficial level, about 'alien' customs and beliefs. Stereotypes, both of people and of their attitudes to life, are more comfortable to live with than the admission that our own habits of thought may be subject to challenge. Instead of celebrating difference, we in the West in particular are perhaps in danger of insisting that other cultures conform to our expectations. We are happy that they should retain a thin veneer of their original features in order to make travelling to foreign countries 'east of Suez' an interesting experience. While 'quaint' customs, ethnic clothing, and scenery unlike ours are all are attractive to us, making an effort to understand the way of thought of those brought up within a totally different cultural framework would be more painful for us, involving as it would a considerable outlay of time and effort and dispelling some comfortable and simplistic misinterpretations.

It is within this context that the 2004 British IBBY conference, 'East meets West in Children's Literature,' can be seen as an attempt to fulfil the hopes of the founder of the International Board on Books for Young People, Jella Lepman, that children's books would be instruments of greater understanding between nations. Her concern had been generated by the clashes between ideologies during the second World War. While today we are faced with even wider areas of mutual incomprehension, children's literature can still be a means of bridging gaps. If young people are made aware of the need to respect the cultures and beliefs of those from different backgrounds, there is hope that they will grow up with a more empathetic response towards other people than is all too evident in the world today.

From at least medieval times, the idea of the 'mystic' East has attracted both western travellers and those who stayed at home and read their accounts of their travels. As Edward Said observes in his influential study, *Orientalism*: 'The Orient was almost a European invention, and had been since antiquity a place of romance, exotic beings, haunting memories and landscapes, remarkable experiences' (1978: 1). The attractive force of this compound of strangeness, fear and fascination, together with the desire to open up new markets for trade, can be seen in the power of legendary writings by and about the Venetian, Marco Polo (1254-1324), and the travels of Sir John Mandeville (c. 1356). The latter blends fact and fantasy in a way that provides early evidence of the craving for the exotic: hippopotamuses and griffins are described in an equally factual manner. The popularity of later British travellers such as Lady Hester Stanhope (1776-1839), Alexander

Kinglake (*Eothen*, 1844), Charles Doughty (*Travels in Arabia Deserta*, 1888), Lawrence of Arabia (1888-1935), Dame Freya Stark (*Baghdad Sketches*, 1933), and Wilfred Thesiger (*Arabian Sands*,1959 & *The Marsh Arabs*, 1966) attests rather to the power of romance about the Arab world and the East, than to any desire on the part of readers for accurate information. Within the literary tradition of books set in 'the orient,' the most notable name must of course remain that of Rudyard Kipling (1865-1936), because of both the quality of his writing and his subsequent influence.

The treatment by speakers at the IBBY conference of the theme East meets West was very varied, but some interesting links appear between papers that at a superficial level might seem to have little in common. Notable amongst these is the difficulty of creating an authentic picture, particularly within the many and diverse burgeoning indigenous children's literatures, of the cultures and individuals depicted, given the way that classics from the western world maintain an enduring power over readers' imaginations. The range of territories discussed in these papers is wide, going beyond those once part of the British Empire. While the term 'East' in the papers which follow is applied in general to lands east of Suez, we have taken some liberties with longitude in order to give a passing mention to some areas not strictly east but treated in literature as equally exotic, notably Africa.

Depiction of the East in English Children's Literature

Edward Said (1978) sees the relationship between East and West as constantly one determined by the power of the latter, so that the 'orient' is always seen in literature through a European prism. He claims that:

> Orientalism can be discussed and analysed as the corporate insitution for dealing with the Orient – dealing with it by making statements about it, authorizing views of it, describing it, by teaching it, settling it, ruling over it: in short, Orientalism as a Western style for dominating, restructuring, and having authority over the Orient. (1978: 3)

The result of this is that the east is often defined in imposed terms, not only for the readers of this western literature but also, as an all too frequent consequence, for the Orientals themselves, which means that children's writers from India and other eastern countries have often tended to see themselves in relation to the tradition of English children's literature.

A further consequence of what Said describes as 'the hegemony [i.e. the predominance of certain cultural forms over others] of European ideas about the Orient, themselves reiterating European superiority over Oriental backwardness' (1978: 7) is that European identity is seen as superior to that of non-European peoples and cultures, and it becomes logical to think of

European literatures as superior to indigenous ones. The implication is that the 'strange', whether in literature or in life, is potentially regarded as inferior, though at the same time exotic.

The effect of such attitudes is to be detected in the children's fiction discussed in some of the papers which follow. One of the earliest children's writers to include an Indian setting in her fiction was the popular and influential Mary Martha Sherwood, who lived in India for some years early in the nineteenth century and in whose work the indigenous people are viewed with a combination of horror at their (to her) repulsive habits, and fascination at their exotic qualities. Her stories however display the conviction that the inevitable triumph of Evangelical Christianity in India will ultimately make the people, in effect, brown-skinned Britons for whom cleanliness is next to godliness. Later writers also display a somewhat attenuated version of such notions, as discussed in my paper in the current volume. We are however fortunate today that the better-informed and less prejudiced work of writers such as Jamila Gavin, discussed here by Sophie Mackay, is more likely to influence young readers' perceptions of India.

The treatment of characters from various parts of the East is considered in the papers by Mary Cadogan and Ann Lazim. Both are uneasy about earlier portrayals of 'exotic' individuals, but it is heartening to see that they have detected progress towards less stereotypical creations in more recent children's literature.

The Development of Non-Western Literatures

As indicated above, a consequence of the 'subaltern' position of children's literatures developing in erstwhile colonial territories is the way in which they tend to see themselves in deference to the Western models, generally that of English. This phenomenon, discussed by Homi BhaBha (1984) in his analysis of what he terms mimicry, is revealed in several of the papers in this collection. Both Gita Wolf and Preetha Leela recall the popularity in India some years ago of children's stories by Enid Blyton and others, while Sandra Williams and Yukie Ito document the problems relating to the creation of an indigenous children's literature in Singapore and Laos respectively.

Gillian Lathey's paper sets this situation into a wider context, while Marian Allsobrook provides an informative survey of the situation within China, with its very different history.

The East in its own voice

Some of the plenary speakers at the conference (Tony Bradman, Tanuja Desai Hidier, Farrukh Dhondy, Bali Rai and Rehana Ahmed, whose views are summarised in the contextual chapter which follows this introduction) spoke of the difficulties facing writers from families of immigrant origin in finding their own voices within Western culture, rather than being spoken for by others. There is also some anxiety involved in the question of the extent to which negative aspects of ethnic minority communities should be portrayed within a society which may already be prejudiced against them.

Nevertheless, while the influence of both contemporary and earlier western children's literature is widespread, it is heartening to realise that it is not seen as always defining those from other cultural areas. Taraneh Matloob's brief account of children's literature in Iran, although it could not be given at the conference itself, provides a valuable reminder of the riches of other cultures.

Japan is a country which has its own cultural modes but has been prepared to make use of Western models to an extent and in a form which has seemed appropriate to Japanese authors. They have however transformed these in a manner not generally possible in those countries which were at some stage European colonies. Lisa Sainsbury's paper serves as a bridge between this autonomous yet intertextual children's literature and the vibrant indigenous artistic genre of the *anime*, the Japanese animated film. The fact that an eminent Japanese creator of anime, Miyazaki, is making use of the fiction of the distinguished British children's writer, Diana Wynne Jones, serves as another example of how literature can bridge cultures.

A celebration of Jones' work, on the occasion of her seventieth birthday, provided the culminating sessions of the conference. All readers of her fantasy would probably agree that the worlds into which she leads them are even stranger than the 'East' appeared to be to early travellers. This collection from the conference therefore aptly concludes with a summary of the appreciations of her work and with a paper by Nikki Humble on its mythic dimension.

We can only hope that the conference, and the papers resulting from it, will serve towards a greater understanding between cultures and more tolerance of the differences between them.

Notes

1. In a paper summarised in the preface 'East Meets West: The Context' which precedes this Introduction

2. Ibid

Bibliography

BhaBha, H (1984) 'Of Mimicry and Man: the Ambivalence of Colonial Discourse' in Rice, P & Waugh, P (eds.) (2nd edition, 1992), *Modern Literary Theory: A Reader*, London: Edward Arnold

Said, E (1985; first published 1978) *Orientalism*, Harmondsworth: Penguin

Part 1

Mostly India

A Hundred Years of Eastern Characters in Popular Children's Fiction

Mary Cadogan

The focus of the discussion in this paper is characters from Asian, African and Afro-Caribbean contexts as encountered in the school story genre. Consideration of the role of such characters is inevitably linked with changes in society in twentieth-century Britain, although authors also realised early on that, with or without social points being made, such characters could have an extremely enlivening effect on their stories. For 'eastern' we could quite often substitute the word 'exotic'. Characters from Asia and Africa often imply an element of fantasy in their depiction, but were sometimes also realistically portrayed. This may have been because of direct contact between the writers and the sons of well-to-do Asian families who came to be educated in English public schools and universities.

However, in many working-class communities during the early decades of the twentieth century, Asian or African people were rarely encountered at first hand. For example, until the Second World War began, as a child in a South East London suburb I had never met a 'coloured' person, or even any kind of 'foreigner', other than a Chinese girl who, brought over by missionaries, attended one of our Sunday School outings. The war years (1939-1945) brought servicemen from Asia, Africa and elsewhere into Britain, as well as refugee adolescent girls from Nazi-occupied Europe who came into my school. Nevertheless 'multi-ethnic' Britain, in the long-term residential sense, only began to establish itself after the ending of the Second World War.

When we consider eastern influences in popular children's fiction, it should be remembered that, with some of the stories under discussion, we are looking back over nearly a hundred years, to a period when attitudes and inter-racial relationships were very different from those which exist today. The accepted images of eastern people came largely from books and, where children were concerned, from comics and weekly story papers. Black and coloured stereotypes were often crudely presented, as indeed were many of the white stereotypes within their pages.

Earlier references to Asian and African characters do occur in other genres (notably in Kipling's stories for adults) but their potential for enriching plots and atmosphere became particularly evident in the Edwardian school stories for boys by Charles Hamilton ('Frank Richards') and P G Wodehouse, as well as those of Henry St John Cooper (who dispensed with 'Cooper' in his school stories and, as 'Mabel St John', also wrote for girls). It is interesting that these stories all originally appeared in the first decade of the century, and in story-papers and magazines rather than in hardback books.

Frank Richards introduced Hurree Jamset Ram Singh, the schoolboy Nabob of Bhanipur, into *Pluck* in 1906 and then, because of this character's popularity, transferred him into the *Magnet* soon after this began in 1908. Hurree then took his place in the Remove Form at Greyfriars where, until Richards died in 1961, he remained near the centre of the action and ethos. His author felt that 'to create a coloured boy on equal terms' with the home-grown manly heroes 'would have a good effect.' On the whole this was true, although there were elements of caricature from time to time in Hurree's personality, and even more in Richards' Chinese schoolboy, Wun Lung. Editors of the *Magnet* and other weekly papers soon realised that to include boy characters from different countries boosted circulation – hence there were plenty of characters from the colonies and dominions where the *Magnet*, *Gem* and *Boys' Friend* were enthusiastically bought and read.

P G Wodehouse, as 'Basil Windham', wrote *The Luck Stone* as a serial for the 1909 *Chums*. Despite its school setting, there is no doubt that this story was largely inspired by Wilkie Collins' *The Moonstone*. Since Collins' book was first published in 1868, tales of sacred jewels or other relics stolen from eastern shrines and taken to England have never ceased to appear. However, *The Luck Stone* is memorable for its introduction into the public school setting of Ram, an Indian pupil who, like Hurree Jamset Ram Singh, is treated by his author (and fellow-pupils) sympathetically and with a robust lack of sentimentality or patronage.

Nevertheless both Hurree and Ram can be criticized as very simplistic character studies, or even parodies. In his celebrated essay, 'Boys' Weeklies' (1940) George Orwell referred to Hurree Singh as 'a Babu character,' while Richard Usborne (1961) categorised Ram as a direct descendant of Harry Bungsho Jabberjee in F Anstey's *Baboo Jabberjee* (1897). Both Hurree Jamset Ram Singh and Ram used extravagantly flowery speech and direly mixed metaphors but these, and other exotic touches, seemed to charm rather than to repel child readers.

Most important of all was the fact that both Frank Richards and P G Wodehouse gave their Indian boys a large measure of courage, both moral and physical, plus shrewdness and insight which cut through many of the problems and difficulties generally besetting schoolboy characters in English fiction. Also, of course, both Hurree and Ram refused to be bullied. In the first Greyfriars story to feature him (*Magnet* No.6, 'Aliens at Greyfriars', 1908), Hurree comes to the study he is to share with Harry Wharton, the hero of the saga, and with Bulstrode, who is known as the Bully of the Remove. Hurree, who is described as slightly built, 'lithe and inscrutable,' immediately surprises Wharton (and, presumably, the *Magnet's* readers) by giving the bully much more than he bargains for. After issuing several insults,

Bulstrode declares that he will not share a study with 'a nigger.' He physically attacks Hurree but:

> The Hindoo straightened up suddenly, and somehow Bulstrode's feet left the floor, and he was whirled round like a sack of coal, and the next instant he was flying headlong through the door ... Hurree Singh, breathing rather hard, but showing no other sign of undue exertion turned to Wharton with a sweet smile. 'I hope you will forgive me for creating the disturbfulness in the sacred apartment of the study,' he said in his soft, purring voice ...

In Wodehouse's *The Luck Stone* (1909) we find similar displays of courage from the Indian pupil, Ram, who often goes where more street-wise boys fear to tread. For example he takes on Mr Spinder, a bullying (and later proved to be a thieving) master, who is cutting school costs by giving the boys inferior and very restricted supplies of food: 'Hon'ble Spinder, you are paid by parents to provide poor boys with good wholesome food, but hoity-toity, what a falling-off is there! Our stomachs groan with beastly pains ...'

Contemporaneously with Hurree and Ram, 'Mabel St John' (whose forte, as 'Henry St John', had hitherto been boys' boarding school tales) created Coosha. This character was the daughter of a Zulu chief and one of the main protagonists in the 'Pollie Green' serials which ran for several years in the *Girls' Friend* from 1908. Coosha's schoolgirl exploits, though bizarre and very much 'over the top,' made many telling points about friendships which, on the surface, seemed unlikely but were actually extremely resilient. Like Frank Richards's and P G Wodehouse's Indian characters, Coosha absolutely refused to be put down or patronised in any way.

When she first joins Nunthorpe School, Coosha has to be dragged screaming into the classroom. Pollie alone realises that she is frightened, and there is an almost immediate understanding between them. Coosha is at first very overdrawn, unutterably wild-eyed and woolly-haired in appearance. She soon becomes, like Pollie, an attractive teenage student and they go together to continue their studies at College. Coosha is victimised there by Miss Trumpinshaw, an officious teacher on whom the Zulu girl avenges herself when helping to organise a charity fête. Miss Trumpinshaw's *pince-nez* and mannish trilby hat emphasise her grimly astringent features. Her ancient black coat and skirt are formidable in cut, and Coosha neatly appends to Miss Trumpinshaw's stalwart rear a prominent notice advertising 'One Kiss – only 3 Pens' [pence]. Predictably, trade is not brisk, but Miss Trumpinshaw has to ward off one unattractive and over-enthusiastic military gentleman. Coosha is always quick to visit terrible retribution on anyone who treats her as an inferior.

The 1920s and '30s saw the proliferation of the boarding school story for both boys and girls, and many further fictional embodiments of pupils from Asia and Africa. For example, there was Ram Dass in T H Scott's *A Hit for Six* (1934), a school story with a *Moonstone* theme. Ram Dass attends Halton School in Yorkshire. He is a distinctly *un*heroic oriental prince who wallops and bullies younger boys and is described as 'a rotter' and 'a sly swine.' However, this 'little Burmese bowls with the easy grace of his kind' and manages to achieve a senior position in the school as a result of his cricketing prowess. His presence there attracts the attention of a strange group of itinerant Indians (who are searching for the Luck Stone, yet another sacred jewel stolen from an oriental shrine!). Ram Dass's standards are so far removed from the (fictional) traditions of schoolboy truthfulness that he fails to own up to breaking bounds at night, even though the headmaster has threatened to punish the whole school if the miscreant does not come forward. Ram Dass dismisses an appeal from Mayne, his only friend, who says:

> My old man would chuck me altogether if I was expelled – ship me off to the colonies or somewhere. It wouldn't make much odds to you, I suppose. You'd be a Rajah in your benighted country just the same if you went back with a dozen murders on your soul. But I didn't hear you own up (Scott, 1934)

Following in Coosha's footsteps came Naomer Nakara, the teenage Arabian Queen who was to adorn and enliven Morcove School in the 1920s and '30s in the weekly *Schoolgirls' Own* in stories by Horace Philips ('Marjorie Stanton'). Naomer's native country was described as 'an Arabian desert kingdom,' and frequently Arab characters played prominent parts in the long-running Morcove saga. Indeed they, and others from what was dubbed 'the mysterious East,' were often featured in school and adventure stories in the Amalgamated Press's between-the-wars girls' papers, *Schoolgirls' Own, School Friend* and *Schoolgirl*. Socially these characters ranged from fabulously rich oriental princesses to poor, subservient South Sea islanders of the 'Me Klistian, me missionary girl' variety.

At Morcove School Naomer is generally described as 'impish'. She is never quite the conventional inmate of most traditional English girls' schools of the period: 'Naomer darling, it isn't usual to eat *all* the sugar out of the sugar-basin!' The Morcove author introduced another Arabian girl, Rose of the Desert, into the stories in 1921. Clad only in wispy and spangled veils, Rose floats in and out of the saga for several years, undaunted by the chilly wind and rain of Morcove's Devonshire moorland setting. She is seeking a sacred lamp which had been stolen from its Arabian home by English explorers, and the Morcove girls soon befriend her. As a result of this relationship they go off to the North African desert for the 'hols' year after year. There, never learning from experience, they suffer the recurring hardships of sandstorms, imprisonment by corrupt 'sultans' and hairs-breadth escapes from death. They do of course have the bonus of seeing amazing desert scenery and the marble minarets, fountains and pools of Naomer's Arabian kingdom.

The boarding school story declined in popularity from the 1950s when the British Empire began to break up, and children were no longer being sent by their parents in far-flung countries to be educated in England. The roles of Asians and Africans in children's stories underwent drastic changes as authors endeavoured to reflect the realities of 'multi-cultural' Britain. Here, of course, we see a very different 'eastern' influence on British school stories. These, in general, had moved by the 1970s from boarding- to day-school settings. Also, school children from India, Pakistan and the West Indies were now homegrown in our society rather than visitors or immigrants. This involved authors in greater understanding of the challenges which these characters – and their white schoolmates – had to face. Authors also needed to probe antagonisms and friendships between children from different ethnic and religious groups.

Two important books to consider in this respect are Gillian Cross's *Save Our School* (1981) and Jan Needle's *My Mate Shofiq* (1978). In her light-hearted but perceptive story, Gillian Cross features Clipper, a West Indian girl who leads a small gang of white boys. (Feminist touches are provided here in the same satisfying and taken-for-granted way that inter-racial friendships are presented.) *My Mate Shofiq* is also particularly worthy of study. It describes the slowly developing friendship between Bernard, an English boy, and Shofiq, a British born Pakistani boy. Jan Needle sensitively shows how this relationship is both threatened and strengthened by challenges presented by school bullies. The book raises many serious questions about modern school communities and does not provide any facile answers. It is a fine example of how the English school story has been affected by what we might now only loosely call 'eastern influences,' and itself has carried the school story into a newer social incisiveness.

Bibliography

Primary Texts

Cross, G (1981) *Save Our School*, London: Methuen

Needle, J (1978) *My Mate Shofiq*, London: Andre Deutsch

Richards, F (1908) 'Aliens at Greyfriars, in *Magnet*, 21st March 1908

St. John, M (1908) 'Pollie Green at Cambridge,' serialised in *Girls' Friend* from 23rd May to 21st November 1908

Scott, T H (1934) *A Hit For Six*, London: Frederick Warne

Stanton, M (1923) 'Morcove in Morocco,' serialised in *Schoolgirls' Own* from 21st April to 19th May 1923

Stanton, M (1921) 'The Vanished Schoolgirls,' serialised in *Schoolgirls' Own* from 24th December 1921 to 21st January 1922

Wodehouse, P G (1997) *The Luck Stone*, London: Galahad Books (Reprinted from the serialisation in *Chums*, 1909)

Secondary Texts

Orwell, G (1940) 'Boys' Weeklies' in *Horizon* magazine, March 1940

Usborne, R (1961) *Wodehouse at Work to the End* London: Herbert Jenkins

Gulmohar Trees and Cream Teas: The Influence Of British Children's Fiction Upon The Indian Psyche

Preetha Leela

> We must do our best to form a class who may be interpreters between us and the millions whom we govern. A class of persons Indian in blood and colour but English in taste, opinions, words and intellect. (Lord Macaulay, 1813)

Today, nearly fifty-eight years after Independence, Lord Macaulay would find it impossible to find a class of young people in India who are totally English in taste, opinions, words and intellect. Independent Indians do not have imposed on them the doctrines that Lord Macaulay laid down for their forerunners. However, the dominance of English fiction over the English-medium school remains unchangingly strong and resolute. Read alongside prescribed texts from India and other countries, characters like those in Blyton's *The Famous Five* are still household favourites.

These favourites which have been passed down from mother to daughter, father to son, sibling to sibling and so on, have yet to be discarded in favour of Indian counterparts. If anything, they have become, in some ways, almost as popular as Indian mythological stories such as the story of 'How Lord Ganesh Acquired an Elephant's Head.'

Looking at the books available in India and in other countries, we know that there is certainly no lack of contemporary Indian writers. Even if we did narrow our browsing to Indian children's fiction, there would not be any dearth of Indian writers. Then how do these British books from the early twentieth century, which have been long succeeded by other writers in their mother country, remain popular? It's simply because these characters from a certain era have been kept alive through sentiment and passed on in a way that has now made them a firm part of a certain society in India - a society in which English is still the predominant language, where the popularity of these British books has not dwindled. Strangely, this is despite a sudden and deliberate increase in the market for Indian fiction for children and young adults.

It's interesting to note the choice and range of fiction available to the Indian child today. Go into 'Good Books,' an exclusive children's bookshop in Chennai (Madras) and you will find scores of books: regional, national and international. Despite the colourful stocks of Indian books, I noticed my old childhood favourites lining the walls equally proudly, seeming almost to revel in the fact that, in this case, being on the shelf meant being evergreen.

Although English books are often read side by side with those of Indian writers, this was not always the case. While Independence brought native literature back to the natives, scores of Indians who had read children's writers like Enid Blyton, Agatha Christie, Frank Richards and so on, clung on to them, ironically with the same zeal with which they embraced Gandhism, Kadhi and the need for 'Freedom' and 'self government'! Needless to say, these books were passed on for generations. Until quite recently, most of the reading material available to children in English-speaking schools had a kind of 'middle-class Englishness' about it. This was certainly true during my own childhood.

I grew up in the post colonial period (which I am not sure is entirely over yet), in a metro then called Madras, now Chennai and famous in Britain for its colonial history as well as for Madras curry powder, an essential ingredient of the modern British kitchen. In my childhood, the dominance of Enid Blyton books in primary school meant that descriptions of food in early childhood compositions were made up of images of cream teas, potted meat and egg sandwiches.

Inspired greatly by the 'St Clare's' series by Blyton, my circle of friends and myself secretly organised a midnight feast during a sleepover and discovered to our horror that egg sandwiches tasted foul hours after they had been made. My sister, who refused to eat hers, remarked that they probably tasted better in English weather where the lack of heat meant that the eggs didn't feel as if they'd been cooked more than once.

At school, the nuns and other teachers occasionally held classes under the orange flowered 'gulmohar' trees. On days when the teachers were weary and the climate was ripe for wandering minds to turn away from academia at the least excuse, we would be given reading practice. We usually liked this, as not only did this mean easy reading, it meant we would have a chance to note everyone's reading voice and to rib them about it later. The teachers usually picked excerpts from Richmal Crompton, Frank Richards, Enid Blyton, Agatha Christie and so on. As entertainment back then was limited to a few hours of television per week, during which we watched popular songs from Indian movies or an odd assortment of foreign imports such as *I love Lucy*, *Father Dear Father*, or *Some Mothers Do 'Ave 'Em*, books and cinema formed our main entertainment, and we discussed these avidly with friends. So if during reading practice, we did come across an extract from a book that we had not read, we would enthusiastically seek it out from the library. If this were part of a secret plan on the teacher's side to get us to improve our reading, it usually worked. Reading as we all know holds an influence on early tastes and perceptions and in this case, its influence was not lost on us.

It was therefore not surprising that our early compositions (as well as some later ones) contained few traces of Krishna, Fatima, rice and dhal, but rather were filled with Mary, Pauline and Julian. Our amateur attempts usually came with all the trimmings of thatched cottages, men in tweeds, ladies in frocks and dialogues charmingly interspersed with 'Oh how simply ripping!'

On the other hand, it would be unfair to claim that there was no Indian writing for children available to us at all, for indeed, there was. One of the books that influenced me enough to turn my studies towards the Indian Independence movement was Shashi Deshpande's *The Narayanapur Incident*. However these books were few and not readily available. Indian Comics on the other hand, such as *Chandamama* and *Amar Chithra Katha* were just as avidly read along with our English favourites.

These comics made Indian myths accessible to Indian children, and indeed, many an Indian child did learn about Ancient India and religion through them. The comics were usually abridged translated versions of Indian myths like the *Ramayan*, and much of the translation was direct from languages such as Sanskrit. But perhaps to a child, no matter how vivid his or her imagination is, remarks like 'Oh blow! The dinner gong's just gone' seem to be more within the realms of reasonable thought than 'Oh illustrious one, thou art deserving of a boon.' Hence, the dominant influence upon our reading remained these English books. Additionally, we were encouraged to read them and many of them were chosen by adults in order to improve our English.

If we at any point lapsed into our mother tongue to discuss movies etc, we were firmly reprimanded and told that we were privileged to be attending an expensive English-speaking school, and must do our best to learn English properly. As an adult, I find the logic behind this somewhat baffling, as I know that it is perfectly possible to be bilingual. However as a child, I immediately shut up when I was scolded for being my natural Indian self for a few snatched minutes in a day.

The sentiment behind our well stocked, albeit far removed from all things Indian, library was that in order for us to learn English properly while at school, we had to read and behave as if we were English. Old habits die-hard and it was a while before we could break free from the moulds of reading, speaking, thinking and writing in a certain culturally artificial way that dominated us for years.

Since India is largely regional-language-based in its education, and less than five percent of the population is English speaking, it would be logical to ask how the influence of this education could extend beyond the few that attended these schools. Although this percentage is small, it amounts however to more than twenty-five million people and these people are the ones who dominate the best jobs and in doing so, very often impose their personal preferences.

Even in extremely regional and nationally led industries like Bollywood, there is a certain subtle influence from early childhood reading, which seems to dominate. Indeed more often than not, the writer or director is an English-medium educated product who belongs to this twenty-five million. Boarding school scenes frequently appear in Bollywood films (another irony is that these are usually shot in Switzerland), Indian ads often contain slightly displaced, subtle allusions to colonial lifestyles, not to mention the fact that several famous, present-day Indian writers have spent a great deal of their childhoods reading very British books. Booker Prize winner Arundhati Roy famously claimed that, unlike other well-known Indian writers, she had never lived in any country other than India and yet even her books have many British references, one of these being to 'Lochinvar' by Sir Walter Scott.

Surely this influence, which even extends to Roy and Seth, must by now have subsided? What about the present generation of Indians who are growing up in a patriotic era where there is a definite tendency to extol the virtues of all things Indian? The bookshops stock children's books that are both Indian and international. However, with every step of technical globalisation, the world is getting smaller and children in India have embraced universally loved children's favourites such as *Harry Potter*. Ironically, once more, this adheres to a certain successful formula for children's books: the boarding school setting.

Lord Macaulay's words may have been forgotten, but even in present-day India, there is an undeniable Englishness about children's reading and writing patterns (although now of course, it is more about modern British children's best-selling writers like J.K Rowling). As an Indian, I feel an enormous sense of pride when I see Indian children's books on the shelves in Indian bookshops, a feeling that is intensified when I see them in Britain. However, I sometimes lament the redundancy of some of my old favourites like Richmal Crompton's William (not that visible in Britain either!).

I am glad I grew up in India reading these very English books and perhaps almost blissfully ignoring my immediate environment of noisy streets, colourful tropical fruits, vegetables and flowers piled high on little carts in markets, auto rickshaws and crowded buses almost comically tilting to one side. However, I am equally glad that Indian children and adults like myself are free of those constraints now. I also hope that, with India having come into its own as a nation of talented adult writers, our children's writers soon emerge as formidable forces and powerfully create images of those noisy streets, colourful markets etc for the British child to escape momentarily from winter nights and temperatures that threaten to plummet to zero!

East Meets West Jamila Gavin's 'Surya' Trilogy

Sophie Mackay

Through its characters and narrative-structure, Jamila Gavin's 'Surya' trilogy explores the complex colonial and post-colonial relationship between Britain and India; the traumatic experience of migration and the struggle of assimilation, and the confusing situation of being split between two different countries. In this paper I shall consider how the structure and narrative style of the texts in the trilogy express the dislocating, disruptive nature of migration experienced by the central characters.

In a very obvious way, Gavin's trilogy is all about East meets West as its protagonists and settings move between England and India. *The Wheel of Surya* (1994), the first text in the trilogy, is set in India and London during the period leading up to Independence and Partition. The narrative traces the journey of a young Sikh brother and sister (Marvinder and Jaspal Singh) from their village in the Punjab to London. The children become separated from their mother (Jhoti) during the destruction of their village in the war between Sikhs and Muslims. They travel to England to find their estranged father Govind, who himself had earlier been encouraged by Harold Chadwick, the resident English schoolteacher in the Indian village, to travel to England for study purposes. On arrival in London, the children discover that their father has rejected his Sikh identity, married an Irish girl (Maeve) and had another child (Beryl). The characters' connection with and movement between India and England is mirrored in the narrative structures of the texts in the trilogy.

In *The Wheel of Surya*, one of the ways in which the experience of migration is communicated is through repeated images of the long white road which leads to the Singhs' village in India. Images of the white road filter into the parts of the narrative which are set in England, linking the characters back with their village in India. The long white road is used as a symbol of migration, of movement away from and towards home. These images appear throughout the trilogy, and are often juxtaposed against scenes which are set in England, as seen in this extract from *The Wheel of Surya:*

> Marvinder looked down Whitworth Road. It seemed to blur and turn into the long white road as she last saw it, stretching out before her filled end to end with creaking bullock carts, and piled with refugees and their belongings. They were refugees again. (Gavin, 1994: 175-176)

Here the image of the white road functions as a liminal space, a form of portal between England and India.

Intertextual references are another way in which the narratives in this trilogy are linked back to India. The link is symbolic of the characters' movement between England and India. In *The Wheel of Surya*, references from the *Rig-Veda* and the *Upanishads* (sacred Hindu texts) occur at the beginning of each of the three sections of the text, creating a frame through which the events in the forthcoming chapters can be seen. The reference to the wandering human soul as an epigraph at the beginning of section two is evocative of the journey upon which Marvinder and Jaspal are about to embark:

> The Wheel of his power made one circle
> In which the human soul was wandering
> Like a restless swan.
> *The Upanishads* (Gavin, 1994: 81)

This extract is also a reference to the title of the trilogy. It refers to the chariot of Surya, the sun god (cf. Gavin, 1994: 95). The image of the chariot is symbolic of the theme of migration which dominates the trilogy.

In *The Eye of the Horse* there is a closer relationship between the pre-chapter intertextual references and the main content of the narrative. Events in the main narrative are loosely paralleled by the story of Rama and Sita. This story comes from the *Ramayana*, which tells of how Sita, Rama's wife, is kidnapped by the evil Ravana and banished to the jungle until Rama, with the help of Hanuman, the monkey god, rescues Sita. Gavin's fictional characters Jhoti, Govind, and Jaspal are linked to Sita, Rama and Hanuman respectively. The story of Rama and Sita is integrated into the main body of the text through individual extracts from the *Ramayana* and through a telepathic dialogue between Marvinder and her mother. In the following extract the dialogue illustrates the way in which Jhoti and Jaspal are allied with Sita and Hanuman:

> Jaspal was fast, elusive and cunning. No one could out run him. It was as if he could make himself invisible.
>
> 'Hanuman, Hanuman,' whispered their mother when Marvinder told her from inside her head. 'Hanuman, the son of Vayu, the God of the wind. He has magic powers – and not even the king of the demons can kill him. Hanuman found Sita. One day, he will find me.'
>
> 'You're like Hanuman,' Marvinder whispered to her brother, when she watched a gang fight on the common. (Gavin, 1995: 29)

The intrusion of Jhoti's voice into the narrative occurs when Marvinder and Jaspal are living in England. Like the intertextual references it is suggestive of the children's division between England and India. Reflecting on her own experience, Nasta (1991: 331) claims that, 'Mother belongs to a culture and a country, which becomes ours, and which gives us our first social identity.' The presence of Jhoti's voice may therefore be seen as representative of Marvinder and Jaspal's connection to India – their motherland.

In this extract the text moves unproblematically between the fantastical nature of the content of the dialogue and the main body of the narrative. This slippage between fantasy and reality produces an effect of magical realism. Chanady writes that, 'In magical realism, the supernatural is not presented as problematic...since it is integrated within the norms of perception of the narrator and the characters in the fictitious world.' (1985: 23-24) The dialogue between Jhoti and Marvinder is integrated into the norms of Marvinder's perception, as she does not reflect on the peculiarity of hearing her mother's voice in her head.

Chanady goes on to say that, ' magical realism belongs neither entirely to the domain of fantasy ...nor to that of reality' (1985: 27). The way in which this text negotiates between fantasy and reality reflects the migrant character's liminal position. Cooper endorses this link between magical realism and the exploration of liminality when she maintains that:

> Magical realism strives ...to capture the paradox of the unity of opposites; it contests the polarities such as history versus magic, the postcolonial past versus the post-industrial present...Capturing such boundaries between spaces is to exist in a third space. (Cooper, 1998: 1)

Here Cooper addresses the question of how magical realism can be used to express the contradictions which exist in liminal spaces. In *The Eye of the Horse,* the use of magical realism is a means of expressing the characters' relationship to two opposing cultures. Boehmer suggests that magical realism is a means of articulating the split perceptions of postcolonial cultures, a claim that supports the notion of a connection between magic realism and liminality:

> Drawing on the special effects of magic realism, postcolonial writers in English are able to express their view of a world fissured, distorted and made incredible by cultural displacement. (Boehmer, 1995: 235).

The following extract from *The Eye of the Horse* reveals the way in which the narrative is disrupted by the fantastical and intertextual nature of the dialogue between Marvinder and her mother:

> 'I made promises. I promised I would wait. I would rather die than go back to our home without my husband and my children.' Jhoti's voice

penetrated her mind with such clarity that Marvinder looked up wondering if anyone heard.

Jaspal suddenly spoke in a low determined voice. 'I wish to go home. It's all I ever wanted. We must go back to our village. We will find out about our mother...'

'Praise be to God,' murmured Jhoti.

There was a long silence, then Govind said quietly. 'That's what I want too. It pleases my heart to hear you say it'

'The monkeys built a bridge. It only took them five days – with the help of the spirits of the ocean, and then they were able to rush across, kill all the demons and rescue Sita. How long will it take you to cross the ocean, Marvinder my child?' Her mother's voice sounded weak.

'Three weeks on the ocean, Ma, and then another few days before we reach our village.'

'Come soon' said Jhoti, fading.

'Is she very sick?' asked Bulbu, as the teacher crouched in the hollow at the woman's side.

'Yes, very sick. If only she would let me take her to the village...'
(Gavin, 1995: 243-4)

By moving the text between India and England, and between fantasy and reality, the intertextual references in this extract disrupt and fracture the narrative.

Ashcroft *et al* (1998) note that magical realism is a device through which the inclusion of mythic or legendary material from local written or oral cultural traditions can be used to 'interrogate the assumptions of Western, rational, linear narrative and to enclose it within...a body of textual forms that recuperate the pre-colonial culture' (1998: 133). In *The Eye of The Horse* the references to the *Ramayana* disrupt the linear flow of the narrative and enable it to enter into a dialogue with an aspect of indigenous Indian culture. This generates a dialogic interchange between pre- and post-colonial cultures.

In addition to the inclusion of the story of Rama and Sita, the narrative of *The Eye of the Horse* is split into three separate strands set in three different locations: London, Delhi, and in or around the village in India. The previous extract, with its telepathic dialogue between Marvinder and Jhoti, shows an example of the split between England, where the beginning of the extract takes place, and India to where, after the interlude of dialogue, the narrative jumps. The split of the narrative into several interrelated strands and locations and its movement between them produces an unsettled, itinerant narrative which reflects Marvinder's and Jaspal's split between two worlds.

In *The Track of The Wind* the narrative is interrupted by references to *Manu's Law* (an early Hindu Code of Law which dates back to the fourth century BC[1]). The following reference to *Manu's Law* occurs on the day of Marvinder's wedding, when Patrick, with whom she fell in love while in London, comes to visit her:

> ...he caught a glimpse of a young woman in red...her slim brown hand raised as if reaching out and an expression on her face ... which told him all he needed to know.
>
> Manu's Law states: *In the fire set at the time of marriage, the householder should perform the domestic rituals and the five sacrifices in accordance with the rules...* (Gavin, 1997: 149)

The way in which this extract from *Manu's Law* is positioned against Patrick's arrival in the village is representative of Marvinder's split between her life in India, which is dictated by rules and tradition, and the freedom of the life she left behind in England. Stephens writes that intertextuality, 'is concerned with how meaning is produced at points of interaction' (1992: 117). The significance of this intertextual interaction is that through juxtaposing two sets of cultural values it expresses Marvinder's division between those two cultures.

The intertextual and multi-stranded nature of the texts in this trilogy creates polyphonic narratives. The three narrative strands in *The Eye of The Horse* introduce voices of various different characters. Similarly, polyphony is generated by the intertextual references as these too introduce voices from different characters, cultures and periods of time, through letters and the indigenous voices alluded to by the Hindu texts.

The disrupted narrative form and conflicting voices of Gavin's 'Surya' trilogy are not only an expression of the protagonists' connection with, and migration between, England and India but also articulate the chaos of post-war Britain and the conflicts in India at the time of independence.

Notes

1. cf. The Concise Mythological Dictionary, 1989, Peerage Books, p104

Bibliography

Primary Texts

Gavin, J (1994) *The Wheel of Surya*, London: Mammoth

Gavin, J (1995) *The Eye of the Horse*, London: Mammoth

Gavin, J (1997) *The Track of the Wind*, London: Mammoth

Secondary Texts

Ashcroft, B Griffiths, G & Tiffin, H (1998) *Key Concepts in Post-Colonial Studies,* London: Routledge

Boehmer, E (1995) *Colonial and Postcolonial Literature*, Oxford: Oxford University Press

Chanady, A B (1985) *Magical Realism and the Fantastic,* New York: Garland

Cooper, B (1998) *Magical Realism in West African Fiction*, London: Routledge

Nasta, S (1991) *Motherlands,* London: The Women's Press

Stephens, J (1992) *Language and Ideology in Children's Fiction*, Harlow: Longman

Exoticism and Evangelism: Mrs Sherwood and Others

Pat Pinsent

> ...the hilly regions where the luxuriant vegetation, the cloudless sky, the slender palm raising its glossy coronal above themore bushy forest trees: the punkah tree ... with its spreading leaf, the Cassia, the Baubool... and the plantain, not more beautiful than profitable: the venerable Banyan, itself a forest, the golden cornfields, the white herds grazing in the meadows, the sacred Brahmin kite soaring in mid-air, the white paddy bird, ... all convey an imperfect idea of what this country might be... and what it shall be, filled with the knowledge of the Lord. (Mary Martha Sherwood)[1]

I have suggested in the Introduction to this volume that perhaps even to a greater degree than writers for adults, authors of fiction for children tend to be affected by what Edward Said (1978) describes as 'Orientalism'. This phenomenon is revealed in aspects of their writing which show an appreciation of what they see as positive features, as well as in the more frequently encountered negative responses to the East. The passage quoted above (not itself written for the young) is representative of the way in which some British travellers were fascinated by the strangeness of their surroundings and the behaviour of the inhabitants; if they communicated this in their books they must have engendered in their readers something of their own delight in the exotic. At the same time, they frequently expressed horror at the differences between on the one hand the poverty and religious practices they observed, and on the other the 'cleanliness next to Godliness' ideal of nineteenth century British middle-class behaviour. Their depictions of India and other countries under the imperialist sway may well have reinforced their English readers' implicit feelings of effortless superiority at themselves being British, Christian and therefore automatically, to Western eyes, rational.

Said's presentation of the pervasive orientalism of Western writers may be summed up as: the East[2] is seen as 'other' and inferior to the west; it is characterised by the worst qualities of humanity, ones which Westerners do not with to recognise in themselves, such as cruelty, sensuality, decadence and laziness; its people are governed by their passions, resulting from their racial origins, rather than acting as individuals (cf. Barry, 1995: 192). All of these aspects are easy to identify in the writings for children of Sherwood and the other writers looked at in this paper. Nowhere are both the negative and the positive aspects of the exotic more notable than among writers who were motivated by the desire to bring the Christian gospel to the East, while not neglecting the equal importance of edifying British children. Such writers often take delight in the strange plants and animals, and the sights which they see as revealing the grandness of God's creative design and providing a foretaste of the delights of paradise[3]. At the same time they display a horror at some of the conditions in these 'pagan' countries, and many evangelical writers relate these to their conviction that the benighted souls of the 'natives' were destined for Hell unless the gospel could be preached to them in time. While the present paper focuses on Mary Sherwood, I shall also mention more briefly some later missionary writers who display some similar tendencies.

Mary Martha Sherwood, who spent several years in India early in the nineteenth century, as an army wife, was probably the most notable Evangelical writer for children. Her almost paradigmatic 'orientalism' is strongly related to her evangelistic sense of mission, which she strove to serve by her own writing, both whilst in India and later in England, and also by being actively engaged in the education of the army children. Today there is no doubt that she, and others like her, would rightly be judged to be 'cultural imperialists,' a term to which might well be added 'religious imperialists.' To view her only in this way however is to downgrade her burning desire to bring salvation, which she saw as exclusively available to those who had accepted Christ as their personal saviour, to the people benighted by paganism. Readers today need constantly to guard against the danger of letting twenty-first century sensibilities about both language and culture affect their responses to the work of writers from the past, who necessarily lacked insights that today seem axiomatic. Before discussing *Little Henry and his Bearer* (1814)[4] in detail, a certain amount of context is necessary, to situate both the author herself and the themes and language in this short novel within the thought of the early nineteenth century.

Sherwood and Evangelical literature for children

The term 'Evangelical', unlike 'evangelistic', which simply denotes a zeal to preach the Christian gospel, was associated, during much of the nineteenth century, with a Calvinistic conviction that even young children should be regarded as miserable sinners, human nature having been totally depraved at the Fall, as a result of original sin. The only chance for human beings was seen as being the admission of their own sinfulness and the attribution to themselves of the merits of Christ's death. A Victorian writer, G W E Russell, remembered from his Evangelical childhood that he was taught:

> that all mankind were utterly sinful, and therefore in danger of Hell; that God had provided deliverance in the atoning death of Christ; and that, if only we would accept the offer of salvation so made, we were forgiven, reconciled and safe.(Quoted in Bradley, 1976: 20)

Given the fallen nature of this world, much the best thing, especially for children, whom the Evangelicals, unlike their contemporaries, Wordsworth and the Romantics, did not regard as innocent) was to die young. This kind of conviction is in a direct line of descent from much seventeenth century Protestant literature. One of the best-known writers from the earlier era is James Janeway, whose *A Token for Children* (1672) recounts the holy deaths of several young children. As Gillian Avery comments: 'Death in a state of grace was what every parent wished for a child, and if it died young it had been put beyond the reach of the evils of this world...' (1989: 107). Such a view lingered on into Victorian times, as demonstrated in several papers in *Representations of Childhood Death* (ed. Avery & Reynolds, 2000) and most vividly displayed in the character of Dickens' Little Nell (*The Old Curiosity Shop,* 1841). The pious and moribund protagonist of Sherwood's *Little Henry* is very much part of a (paradoxically!) living tradition.

Mary Martha Butt was born in 1775, the daughter of a clergyman. She read widely and wrote stories, and taught Sunday school before marrying her cousin Captain Henry Sherwood in 1803. Not long afterwards, she went to India, leaving their eldest daughter behind in England. She had two further children out there, Henry and Lucy, both of whom died, though the Sherwoods had other children later, to whom they gave the same names. As a mother of young children in a climate where the health of Europeans was always at risk, she was inevitably horrified at alien hygienic practices, while her association of these very often with the forces of evil is scarcely surprising given her religious beliefs, which saw no good in any religion other than Evangelical Christianity.

While she was in India, Sherwood had the experience of meeting the children of army personnel, and this caused her great concern about what she saw as their inadequate religious instruction, both in their homes and in army schools. She herself founded schools, and wrote a catechism to further their instruction. During this period she wrote the manuscript of *Little Henry*, sending it home to her sister, Lucy Cameron, also a writer for children, who was instrumental in getting it published by the Houlston company in 1814. It can perhaps be seen as within the Evangelical tradition of putting forward heroic lives for emulation; since her target was young children, the edifying life of a young child fulfilled this objective most effectively. She also started to write her best-known work, *The History of the Fairchild Family* (first published in 1818) while she was in India[6]. The deaths of young children are important in this book too, one providing a dreadful warning and the other an edifying example. While *Little Henry* was not Sherwood's first work of fiction[7], it certainly became one of her most popular and, with the subsequent *Fairchild Family* achieved a considerable number of editions throughout the nineteenth century. She returned to England in 1816, carrying on her literary work, which included a sequel (1842) to *Little Henry*, continuing the story of his Bearer, Boosy. In due course she became less exclusive in her Calvinist beliefs; Harvey Darton (1910: xii) notes that in 1833, after the death of her daughter Emily, she reached the view that 'salvation was wholly unconditional, a free gift of Divine love. ' She died in 1851.

At the period when Sherwood was in India, many Christians felt frustrated at being denied the opportunity to preach Christianity to the 'natives'. In his study of the British Empire, Niall Ferguson talks of the policy of the East India Company of religious toleration towards indigenous Indian religions, even if, as he says, this policy arose more out of pragmatism than principle (2003: 137). Laurence James, in *Raj: the Making and Unmaking of British India,* sets the religious situation in an historical context, and refers to the fear held by early nineteenth century administrators that Christian missionaries might set the Hindus and Moslems against each other: a mutiny in 1807 was attributed to the effect of missionaries preaching to the sepoys. As a result, chaplains were banned from contact with the Indians, and the entry of missionaries was restricted (1997: 223-4). In 1813, just around the time that Sherwood was writing *Little Henry*, the East India Company's charter came up for renewal and the Evangelicals were pressing for a change of policy about the entrance of missionaries to India.[8] So Sherwood was writing on a very contemporary issue. Her concern can be recognised in her journal: she voices her 'extreme horror' that British officers had to attend 'heathen and Mahometan religious services' (*Life*[9], p252). As will be seen from some of the extracts below, in *Little Henry* she reveals her hostility to the idea that 'one religion is as good as another', a thought she attributes to both of her main characters at different stages before their conversions (*Little Henry,* pp443 & 451). It is against this background that we should see her unwillingness to allow any merits to Indian culture.

Sherwood's Autobiographical Material

Throughout her life, in keeping with the Evangelical tradition of self-examination of conscience[10], Sherwood meticulously kept a journal. F J Harvey Darton's *The Life and Times of Mrs Sherwood* (1910) is compiled from her autobiography, published in 1854 together with previously unpublished extracts from her journals. He interposes a certain amount of editorial material to provide context, but states that her actual words are quoted verbatim, together with, in some places, material from Captain Sherwood, clearly indicated. All the passages from his book which I have used are Sherwood's own, rather than her husband's or Darton's.

The positive tone of the passage quoted at the beginning of this paper contrasts considerably with many of Sherwood's other reactions to the unfamiliar setting. She speaks of:

> Horrible figures of the gods, human beings showing horrid passions, miserable and depraved cripples, dying by slow famine and disease, squalid infants who have never felt the soothings of a mother's love...

> diabolical instruments... obscene religious rites... wanton laughter...(*Life*, p316)

Many of these horrors, she deduces are:

> the miserable effects of a false religion... Old women ... are fearful to look upon, their skin is shrivelled and hanging loose... without hope... Secret cruelties which abound in any heathen land... the effect of those abominable creeds which we think it an act of charity not merely to tolerate but to patronise...(*Life*, p252)
>
> ...The abominable adminstrators of a corrupt worship have a much stronger ... influence over the minds of the weaker than the stronger sex. [Some women] the dirtiest I ever saw in India [do not wash but wear jewellery. There is] vile passion on the countenance of almost every person. (*Life*, p280)

It is not difficult to associate the passion of her language with the features that Said claims for 'orientalism'; Sherwood obviously feels that the worst qualities of humanity abound in the people she has seen. What distinguishes her gaze from that of secular writers about India is her identification of such qualities with 'heathen' religion – an aspect which in itself could be seen as hopeful, for once these people are granted enlightenment they may be presumed to have as much potential as their European counterparts.[11]

Sherwood has little appreciation of even the most splendid Indian buildings (as distinct from those erected by the Raj administrators), using the disorganised structure, so different from the houses she would have known in England, as a symbol for the disorder of the country. The palace of a Nawab 'looks like an irregular heap of old castellated buildings arranged without any order'(*Life*, p289) with 'vast and gloomy courtyards, and buffoons ... attempting ... to be what no black man is, witty and amusing.'(*Life*, p293). With our modern sensibility, it is difficult to pardon this last somewhat cynical expression of racism, while Sherwood's distaste at, and unwillingness to attempt to comprehend, what she saw as a false religion are also evident:

> The Hindu saints are usually the most depraved and filthy specimens of the human race, being often daubed from head to foot with mud and mire, their hair long unkempt, and matted with grease and filth. In many instances these wretches are entirely without clothes and as utterly disgusting in speech and manner as in appearance. (*Life*, p317)

Elsewhere she encompasses Islam in her dislike,' The fakirs (or Mussulman saints) and yogis (or Hindu saints) [are] extraordinary... horrid... by wigs and false beards of matted hair and a thick plaster of cow dung [and deformed limbs]' (*Life*, p374). It may be conjectured that her hostility towards the 'holy men' of both faiths springs not only from her horror at their dirt, which she equates with post-lapsarian depravity rather than with godliness, but also from the use of the term 'saints', which she would have seen as papist, contradicting her Evangelical beliefs about the state of humanity as a result of the Fall.

Language

The language of *Little Henry* represents a not insignificant aspect of its exoticism. Even in the late eighteenth century, the English language was developing its pivotal role in the evolution of the Indian linguistic situation; though it is not relevant here to explore the complexity of the reception of English there, its result today is reflected in the estimate that 'there are now more speakers of English in India than in Britain, about seventy million' (McCrum, Cran & MacNeil, 1987: 22). That Indian English is today a vigorous and distinctive form of the English language is proven by the considerable success of authors such as Salman Rushdie, Anita Desai, Vikram Seth and Arundhati Roy, among others.

From the sixteenth century onwards, however, vocabulary interchange has been a two-way traffic, to the extent that some words derived from India, such as 'bungalow' and 'verandah', now scarcely seem exotic at all. Writing early in the nineteenth century and for young readers, Sherwood evidently found it necessary to highlight some of the loan words by italicising them, and in most instances providing an English translation, so that her work attests to the degree of familiarity of certain words that she, or her publishers,[12] considered didn't need translation. Notable among these untranslated words are 'palanquin', the date of incorporation into English of which the Oxford English Dictionary gives as 1588, 'rajah' (1555) and 'sahib' (1627, though she does translate 'choota sahib', 'little master'). Other than those instanced above, *Little Henry* includes, on my count[13], one italicised Indian word of sixteenth century adoption, 'bazar'; twelve of seventeenth century; and eight from the eighteenth century.[14] The single nineteenth century adoption is 'panjammahs', though Sherwood's use of 'bearer' as personal servant is contemporaneous with the date of the novel. There are also nine words which appear not to have been subsequently adopted into British English.[15]

There is no doubt that Sherwood's use and explanation of terms relatively unfamiliar to many of her readers must have added to the appeal of her work. It forms a substantial part of her exoticism, for the words portray objects, people and customs then strange to many readers, such as hookahs, punkahs and pyjamas. Such usage is relatively 'value-free', without the explicit disapproval of her fuller descriptions.

Little Henry and his Bearer

The simple plot of this short novel centres on an orphaned child, who, in the absence of any relatives, is brought up by a rather worldly woman who generally neglects him, leaving him to the care of a Hindu 'bearer', Boosy:

> ...for some years the little child had no other friend than his *bearer*. Boosy never left his *choota sahib* except for two hours in the twenty-four when he went to get his *khauna*... Henry could not speak English, but... he knew every word, good or bad, which the natives spoke. He used to sit in the *verandah*, between his *bearer's* knees, and chew *paun* and eat *bazar* sweetmeats. He wore no shoes nor stockings, but was dressed in *panjammahs,* and had silver *bangles* on his ancles [sic]...He used to see his *bearer* and the other natives performing *poojah*, and carrying about their wooden and clay Gods, ... he also believed that the river Ganges was a Goddess, and that the water of the river could take away sins. He believed too that the Mussulmauns were as good as Christians, for his mamma's *khaunsaumaun* had told him so.[16] (*Little Henry*, pp442-3)

This passage reflects both the devotion of the bearer, and the 'pagan' situation of little Henry, recalling that of many of the children whom Sherwood had met. This comprised not only their 'false' beliefs but also a state of religious indifferentism, of thinking all religions equally good, aspects clearly reflected here in Henry's beliefs and attitudes. The unsatisfactory nature of his beliefs is associated with his 'unEnglish' clothes, his use of 'bad' 'native' words, and his eating of snacks which may be presumed to be unhealthy. Coupled with the fascination at the strangeness, there is the expectation that the reader will be horrified at seeing an English child in this kind of situation.

Fortunately for Henry, and in due course for Boosy, a young lady who has come out to India to marry an Englishman, Mr Baron, stays at Henry's mamma's house and teaches the child:

> ... the lady had brought Henry to know that he and all the world were sinners, and that the punishment of sin is eternal death; and that it was not in his power to save himself, nor for any thing on the earth to wash him from his sins; ... her next lesson was to explain to him what the Lord Jesus Christ had done for him: ... Little Henry was particularly pleased whenever he heard of our Saviour, and by divine grace his heart seemed to be wonderfully filled with love for his Redeemer... his whole behaviour was altered... He would return the *salam* of the poorest *coolie* in the *bazar*. If any body had given him a *rupee* he would not spend it in sweetmeats or playthings; but he would change it into *pice,* and give it to the *fakeers* who were blind or lame, or such as seemed to be in real distress... (*Little Henry*, p446)

The transformation in Henry's behaviour is immediate, and significantly includes abjuring typically Indian objects.

Henry becomes so fervent in his religious practice that he tries to convert Boosy. He prays:

> O Lord God, hear the humble prayer of a poor little sinful child. Give me power, O God... to turn the heart of my poor *bearer* from his wooden Gods and to lead him to the cross of Jesus Christ. (*Little Henry*, p451)

He attempts to discuss religion with Boosy but the bearer argues:

> 'There are many brooks and rivers of water, but they all run into the sea at last; so there are a great many religions, but they all lead to heaven... and one way is as good as another' ... He asserted also, that if he were to commit the greatest sin, and were to go immediately afterwards and wash in the Ganges, he should be quite innocent. (*Little Henry*, p451)

Boosy's assertion reflects the 'indifferentism' which in her journal Sherwood so deplored in the colonial administrators.

Henry is advised by a devout Englishman, Mr Smith, to instruct Boosy how to read the scriptures in his own language, in Persian characters, rather than to argue with him. During the next year, Henry becomes ill; he is joyful at the approach of death, especially when Boosy says 'I wish I could believe in the Lord Jesus Christ' (*Little Henry*, p459). As the child dies, his 'mamma' repents of her worldly ways and begins to read the Bible daily, while after Henry's death Boosy 'renounced *cast* and declared himself a Christian...he was baptized; and continued till his death (which happened not very long after) a sincere Christian... to whom the Christian name of John was given' (*Little Henry*, p461). A monument is erected over little Henry's grave, with the words, ' "*He which converteth the sinner from the error of his way, shall save a soul from death and shall hide a multitude of sins*" [James v.20]' (*Little Henry*, p461). Though 'the damp of that climate has ...defaced the inscription ... the dear child has himself received *an inheritance that fadeth not away* [1Peter i.4]' (*Little Henry*, p461).

It is fairly typical of this kind of devotional writing that Boosy himself should not live long after his conversion. Presumably, like repentant sinners who may lack moral fibre, the Indian bearer may not have the strength to continue in his profession of Christianity amid all the temptations to which he is exposed, so that it is safer that he, like his mentor, dies swiftly. The adoption of a 'Christian' name is also a frequent feature in both fact and fiction.

It would however give a false impression of this novel not to talk about the more attractive features of its exoticism, of which the positive aspects are more numerous than in Sherwood's journals. Such descriptions, like the journal passage quoted at the beginning of this paper, clearly indicate her desire to transmute what she sees as the good features of India into a Christian perspective, while presumably discarding those which cannot be so transformed.

We see how Henry's adopted mother has taken on Indian customs which are associated with indolence (remember the decadence and laziness which Said sees as features of Orientalism) and not consonant with Sherwood's 'Protestant ethic':

> Sometimes his mamma would let him eat his *tiffin* with her: but as she always employed herself at table... in smoking her *hookah,* ... the *tiffin*-time was very stupid to the little boy... there was in general nothing to be heard...but the creaking of the *punkah* and the guggling of the water in the *hookah*...(*Little Henry*, p451)

Shortly after this scene, an almost idyllic vision is created, though it is carefully inserted into Henry's Christian interpretation of what he sees:

> Once it was in one of those lovely places near the *Raja-mehal* hills, Henry and his *bearer* went to walk...Henry could not but admire the beautiful prospect which was before them. On their left hand was the broad stream of the Ganges winding round the curved shore, till it was lost behind the *Raja-mehal* hills. The *budgerow*, gaily painted, was fastened to the shore just below them; and with it many lesser boats, with thatched and sloping roofs. The *dandies* and native servants, having finished their day's work, were preparing their *khauna*, in distinct parties, according to their several *casts* [sic], upon the banks of the river: some grinding their *mussala*, some lighting their little fires, some washing their brass vessels, and others sitting in a circle upon the ground smoking their cocoa-nut *hookahs*. Before them was a beautiful country abounding with corn-fields, *topes* of trees, thatched cottages with their little bamboo porches, plantain and palm trees; beyond which the *Raja-mehal* hills were seen, some bare to their summits, and others covered with *jungle*, which even now afford a shelter to tigers, rhinoceroses, and wild hogs... Henry said, 'Boosy... this would be a very good country, if the people were Christians. Then they would not be so idle as they now are; and they would agree together, and clear the *jungles*, and build churches to worship God in. It will be pleasant to see the people, when they are Christians, all going on a Sunday morning to some fair church built among those hills, and to see them in an evening sitting at the door of their houses reading the *shaster* – I do not mean your *shaster*, but our *shaster*, God's book.' (*Little Henry*, pp452-3)

The contrast between the undesirable idleness displayed not only by the 'natives' but also by the British woman who has adopted their customs, and the energy which, through the child protagonist, Sherwood seems to be advocating, is very apparent. The fierce animals which inhabit the jungles, sadly left uncleared by the 'natives', may again be seen as symbolic of the evil of their religion. But at the same time Henry, whose opinions serve as a guide to the young reader, sees the potential of both the country and the natives, while the exotic features of the scene, a 'beautiful prospect,' where there is a balance between the familiar and the unfamiliar, are memorable and serve to convince the reader of the inherent God-given goodness of the country.

The character of Little Henry himself is based on Sherwood's own son as she hoped he would have developed. Her journals reveal the people she knew who were the inspiration for her characters: Henry Martyn, a man she much admired, was the original for Mr Smith[17], and a young woman who had gone out to India to get married was the original for the 'young lady' who taught Henry and became Mrs Baron (though it is to be suspected that Sherwood also saw herself in this role). These two British characters in the novel are uncorrupted by the 'pagan' and degenerate ways of the land, unlike Henry's mamma, and Mr Smith's wife.

The book has a fairly even balance between the Exotic, displayed in both the beauty and the horror, and signalled clearly in the way the unfamiliar language is emphasised by annotations at foot of page, and the Evangelical, which comes through in Sherwood's burning desire both to convert the heathen and to ensure that British children in India are brought up as Christians. At times it appears that her fascination with the country, evidenced also by her own diaries, almost mutes her message, but on the whole the didacticism triumphs. The deceptiveness of the apparent simplicity of her approach is displayed particularly towards the end of the book, where she speaks in the first person, thus adding an element of authenticity, especially as it is set in a place where she had once lived. The narrator makes the observation of Little Henry's grave appear as her own: 'When I first visited Berhampore, I went to see little Henry's monument,' while she cites Mrs Baron and Mr Smith as authorities for the rest of the story. (*Little Henry*, p461). In her study of Sherwood, Nancy Cutt reveals that as recently as 1967 an editor took the story, together with its sequel giving more details about Boosy's conversion, as fact (1974: 117).

The Last Days of Boosy (1842) expands on the details of Boosy's conversion, for which no doubt many readers must have found the terse summary at the end of *Little Henry* tantalising. It is presented in the form of a correspondence between Mr McNeil, who voices his curiosity about the circumstances in which Boosy became a Christian, and Theophilus Smith, who claims to have known him during this period, and also presents a first person narrative from the bearer himself. The second part is longer than the first, perhaps reflecting Sherwood's greater literary sophistication by that stage of her life. She tells a complex story of how Boosy becomes Bearer to another little boy but is horrified at the contrast in character between this boy and his earlier charge. Boosy also suffers from the calumnies of a Moslem Ayah, who accuses him of being a thief. Gradually he comes to believe in the one God, but is reluctant to admit his faith publicly. At about the same time, his own son dies and he is left to look after his grandson, to whom he gives the name Henry. Mr Smith appears on the scene in the nick of time and arranges for Boosy's baptism, shortly before his death, being left as the guardian of the grandson. I suspect that the extension of the narrative would have had less appeal for children, lacking the attractive figure of the first little boy, and with rather more evangelism than exoticism.

The success of *Little Henry*

In her study of Victorian fiction, J S Bratton describes *Little Henry* as 'epoch-making... one of the first of the new tracts to mingle fictional appeal effectively with the lessons it taught.' Bratton sees its exotic elements as important to this success, 'setting the figure of the pretty neglected child... in the midst of picturesque physical peril,' thus 'evoking pathos as well as an heroic dimension,' especially as Little Henry in his missionary activity is no older than the implied readers (1981: 54). Since the success of this book encouraged Sherwood to write *The Fairchild Family,* it can also be seen as instrumental in what Nancy Cutt describes as turning 'the Evangelical penetration of the nursery that began in 1814 with *Little Henry* into a prolonged occupation' (1974: 63).

The influence of this book was also significant in pioneering the use of India as a setting; Robert Butler notes that 'according to Kipling, Sherwood's book popularized India for Englishmen who "...came to an India ... of palmyra-tree and rice, the India of the picture books, of *Little Henry and His Bearer,* all dead and dry and baking heat"' (1984: 441). Another successor noted by Butler is Helen Bannerman's *Little Black Sambo* (1899). Neither of these writers is relevant to this paper, however; I want rather to focus briefly upon two British missionary writers who display some similar features to Sherwood, in one instance well into the twentieth century.

Charlotte Tucker: A Lady of England (A.L.O.E.)

A later nineteenth century Evangelical writer, Charlotte Tucker (1821-93), who published under the name of A.L.O.E., A Lady of England, was a prolific children's author, producing more than one hundred and fifty books.[18] She was born in England, but before her birth her father had worked in India for 30 years, a fact which fired her with enthusiasm to become a missionary there. She finally achieved this aim in 1875, attracting some surprise at the arrival there of an unattached woman at an age when many missionaries might rather be considering returning to England. India had always formed a prominent theme in her writing; 'Edith and her Ayah' (the title story of a collection by that name published in 1872, though the story first appeared in 1867) presents a not dissimilar situation to that of Little Henry. When the child and her carer are lost in the jungle and confronted by the danger of being killed by a tiger, the Ayah panics, but the little girl prays to God for help. The result is that the tiger is killed by Edith's father who unexpectedly arrives at the scene, and the Ayah becomes a Christian, having been impressed by the power of prayer!

However, a later text, the title story of *In the Spider's Web* (1887), suggests that once there, Tucker was impressed by the extent to which Christianity in India had come of age. The story tells how an Indian Christian girl reconverts a worldly English woman who has lost her faith. In an earlier story, 'A New Way of Eating Plantains' (in *Pomegranates from the Punjab*, 1878), Tucker reveals her desire for the Christian Indians to be their own people, rather than apeing European dress and manners. An elderly Indian woman reminds a younger convert that when people eat fruit, they reject the parts that are inedible; she uses this as an allegory to persuade the younger women to retain the dress of her own people, while accepting the gospel from the Europeans.

The attraction of A.L.O.E.'s work, which was in 1886 ranked high in a survey of the reading of teenage girls,[19] rests partly on its Evangelical vision, which would have recommended it to many Victorian parents as suitable reading for their children. In this aspect there seems little doubt that Tucker was influenced by Sherwood. As well as kindred themes in her work, it is interesting to note that the first story in her *Pomegranates* volume, 'The Two Pilgrims to Kashi,' features a young Hindu boy, Ganesh, who is attracted to Christianity by an encounter with an English boy named Henry (1878: 28). From the young reader's point of view, however, her portrayal of the exotic was probably more significant. Far more of her output than of Sherwood's is set in India – scarcely surprising since she spent twice as long there, and had also created Indian settings long before her departure from England. Unlike Sherwood, Tucker does not italicise unfamiliar words, but she does provide footnotes for terms such as 'chapattis' and 'puja'. Her hostility to Hinduism and Islam is no less than Sherwood's, but she does find some potential virtues in Sikhism:

> Sikh religion is far purer than that of the Hindus, but has unhappily become much corrupted by its professors mingling with the idolators around them... The Sikh religion is more friendly than the Mahomedan, more manly than the Hindu. (*Little Bullets from Batala*, 1880: 74-5)

Thus, in her words of guarded praise, A.L.O.E. reveals a degree of prejudice and a reluctance to find out more about the culture of the people she is living among, comparable to those displayed much earlier by Sherwood.

Gerard Scriven and *Wopsy*

Most of the surviving nineteenth century religious writing, much, though not all, by women Evangelical writers,[20] tends to focus on social conditions in Britain rather than abroad. Evangelical missionary writing carried on, but early in the twentieth century a greater awareness grew of the potential equality as children of God of people of all races.[21] The trappings of colonialism and of religious imperialism were not however easy to discard, and 'orientalism' of the kind seen in Sherwood and Tucker is still prevalent in missionary writing even later in the twentieth century.

Gerald Scriven was a Roman Catholic missionary who belonged to the Missionaries of Africa[22]. In this context it is interesting to note that during the late nineteenth and early twentieth centuries, missionary literature for children formed a substantial part of the religious publishing of another colonising power, Belgium, though of course the missionaries concerned in this instance were members of Roman Catholic religious orders. Scriven is as fervent as Sherwood was in his desire to convert the heathen, though he would have deplored Sherwood's Calvinistic theology. Like her he is fascinated by 'exotic' elements, so that *Wopsy: The Adventures of a Guardian Angel* (published in Patna,1945) complies well with Said's descriptions of the characteristics of orientalism.

The location of the book is an African pagan village abutting on the jungle, though the first scene is in heaven where a young angel Wopsy (whose real angel name would apparently be difficult for the child reader) is set to guard one of the babies. This delights the angel, as he loves them 'because they had big white eyes and such a beautiful shiny black skin' (1945: 8). The baby has a difficult Pagan name but Wopsy calls him Shiny, until later in the book where somehow he manages to get the child baptised, when he is in danger of death. He is given the name John (echoes of Boosy!). Figures of gods in old trees and devils and lions in the jungle abound, but in the end the reader learns that missionaries are coming to the village 'to teach the people about God and to make them happy now and when they are dead and ... they would also look after the sick and teach the children to read and write' (1945: ch.xiii). It is no surprise that at the end Shiny John is going to become a priest, a note which chimes in with the perceptions of both Sherwood and Tucker that once the heathen are converted, they can be as good Christians as the Europeans.

Scriven's book reflects the still existing religious imperialism of its period; for instance, during the 1940s, a project enabled Catholic school children in

Britain to pay a small sum of money towards the missions and choose the name for a baby 'rescued' from paganism. A consequence of this endeavour has been an abundance in missionary territories of Theresas and Bernadettes! Even from this brief description of *Wopsy* it should not be difficult to recognise how in this book the pagan world is depicted as 'other', while the darker elements of human behaviour are 'projected' on to non-Christians, who are classified in group rather than individual terms. Evangelism, as distinct from Evangelicalism, is also strongly apparent in Scriven's approach.

Conclusion

The perspective of this paper has deliberately been confined to the past, to periods when, unlike today, there was an abundance of explicitly Christian didactic texts for children. Religion today figures in quite different ways. On the one hand, several twentieth and twenty-first century writers (such as C S Lewis, Philip Pullman, G P Taylor, Jeanne du Prau and Ben Jeapes) have set their treatment of religious belief into a fantasy framework, which by its nature precludes the kind of issues on which I have concentrated here. Nevertheless there have been a number of Evangelical fiction writers[23], most of whom tend however have not chosen 'exotic' subjects. An exception to this is the prolific writer, Patricia St John, whose *I Needed a Neighbour* (London: Scripture Union, 1987) is set in an unnamed African country; while portraying the hardship of the life of refugees there and certainly putting forward an Evangelical approach to religion, the book shows little evidence of the mixture of horror and fascination so characteristic of the writers discussed above.

I suspect nevertheless that Said's detection of 'orientalism' in so many people who have written about 'the exotic East' suggests that similar attitudes may still be under the surface in many people today who pay lip service to equality. The analysis of work from the more remote past, in which negative perceptions are much easier to detect than in writers whose preconceptions we may share, has the value of helping today's readers to understand their own attitudes and the legacy of empire. Additionally, however much we may deplore their colonial assumptions, the enterprise of missionary writers from the nineteenth century involves much that is worthy of admiration.

Notes

1. Quoted in N Royde Smith, *The State of Mind of Mrs Sherwood*, 1946: 10-11.

2. The term 'East' in effect also includes Africa – even those regions not literally west of Europe.

3. Andrew Marvell (1621-78) expresses a similar concept in his poem 'Bermudas', when he gives a voice to Puritan exiles from England who see the islands as an earthly paradise where they hope to find a natural temple in which to praise God.

4. Subsequently abbreviated throughout this paper to *Little Henry*. Page references to this text are to the 1984 reprint.

5. See Bradley (1976: 146) for instances of this tradition.

6. Both these books, and much of the rest of Sherwood's extensive output, can be seen within the context of the numerous manuals on conduct produced during this period (see Bradley, 1976: 148). With some arithmetical exaggeration, Bradley describes *The Fairchild Family* as 'infinitely the most popular children's book in the first three decades of Victoria's reign' (1976: 186).

7. Before leaving England, she had published *Susan Gray*, about a pious servant girl who dies an early and holy death, and in India she also produced adaptations of Bunyan's *Pilgrim's Progress*, one of these being especially for Indian children.

8. Their eventual success in this aim may partially be attributed to their infiltration of the East India Company (see Bradley 1976: 82).

9. References throughout are to F J Harvey Darton's *The Life and Times of Mrs Sherwood* (1910), abbreviated to *Life*.

10. See Bradley (1976: 23) for details about other writers and how their journals reveal this self-scrutiny.

11. The description in some respects parallels those of other, later, nineteenth century writers, such as Gaskell, observing the degradation forced by poverty and inhumane conditions on the inhabitants of the new industrial cities of the North of England. Presumably, at least at the period when she was writing, Sherwood had had no opportunity to witness such conditions in a 'Christian' country!

12. It is impossible to determine whether the impulse to italicise such words and to provide footnotes came from the author or her publishers, Houlstons, but either way it indicates something of the lack of familiarity of these words.

13. Since some words occur more than once, while some compound words are italicised even though one part of the word is familiar, it is impossible

to exclude an element of subjectivity in estimating these. Spelling throughout is Sherwood's.

14. Seventeenth century: pice [pence], fakeers, punkah, gooroo, shaster [holy book], zemeendar [landholder], puckar, paun, salam, coolie, rupee, dandy; eighteenth century: budgerow [barge], tiffin, hookah, jungle, verandah, bangles, bearer.

15. 'choota' [little], 'khauna' [food], 'poojah' [ceremony], 'khaunsaumaun' [house steward], 'chooteebebee' [young lady], 'sais' [horse servant], 'matre' [sweeper], 'mussala' [spice], 'willaet' [European], though I am sure that the third and eighth of these are generally familiar today in British English.

16. Here and elsewhere the italics are Sherwood's.

17. Martyn translated the New Testament into Urdu (Bradley 1976: 76), so the incident in *Little Henry* where Mr Smith recommends that Henry teach Boosy to read the Bible in his own language clearly marks Sherwood's dependence on real events.

18. For much of the information about A.L.O.E. and her works, I am indebted to the unpublished MA thesis (1999) of Katie Day, and her short article in *The Big Issues* (2001). Day's work gives a good deal of attention to aspects of 'orientalism' in Tucker's fiction.

19. Day (2001: 74), citing Avery, *Childhood's Pattern* (Hodder, 1975: 221)

20. Notable among these are Sarah Trimmer (1741-1810), Lucy Cameron (1781-1858), Charlotte Tonna (1790-1846) and Hesba Stretton (1832-1911). The most prominent among children's religious writers with a High Church background is Charlotte Yonge (1823-1901), while several Roman Catholic writers produced fiction in tract form designed to counter anti-Catholic propaganda.

21. The London Missionary Society, a Protestant body, for instance in its annual report in 1913 emphasised that God did not recognise racial distinctions. (See Sandy Brewer, 2005 for more detail.)

22. At that time, and until near the end of the twentieth century, they were generally known as the White Fathers; though this name was intended as a reference to their habit rather than their race, it gradually has become less acceptable.

23. See for instance 'Evangelistic school stories' in (ed.) Sue Sims & Hilary Clare, *The Encyclopedia of Girls' School Stories*, Aldershot: Ashgate (2000) for a discussion of some of these.

Bibliography

Primary Texts

A.L.O.E. [Charlotte Tucker] (n.d., first published 1878) *Pomegranates from the Punjab*, London: Gall & Inglis

A.L.O.E. (n.d., first published 1880) *Bullets from Batala*, London: Gall & Inglis

Darton, F J Harvey (ed.) (1910) *The Life and Times of Mrs Sherwood (1775-1851)*, London: Wells Gardner Darton & Co.

Scriven, G F (1945) *Wopsy: The Adventures of a Guardian Angel*, Patna: Catholic Book Crusade

Sherwood, M M (1984; first published 1814) *Little Henry and his Bearer*, in Bator, R (ed.) *Masterworks of Children's Literature*, vol.4, New York: Allen Lane with Stonehill Publishing company for Chelsea House Publishers.

Sherwood, M M (n.d., first published 1818) *The History of the Fairchild Family: or The Child's Manual*, London: Ward Lock

Sherwood, M M (n.d., after 1842) *Little Henry and his Bearer* [including *The Last Days of Boosy*] London: Houlston

Secondary Texts

Avery, G 'The Puritans and their Heirs' in Avery, G & J Briggs (1989) (eds.) *Children and their Books: A Celebration of the Work of Iona and Peter Opie*, Oxford: Clarendon Press

Avery, G & Reynolds, K (eds.) (2000) *Representations of Childhood Death*, Basingstoke: Macmillan

Barry, P (1995) *Beginning Theory: An Introduction to Literary and Cultural Theory,* Manchester: University Press

Bradley, I (1976) T*he Call to Seriousness: The Evangelical Impact on the Victorians*, London: Jonathan Cape

Bratton, J S (1981) *The Impact of Victorian Children's Fiction,* London: Croom Helm

Brewer, S (2005) 'From Darkest England to *The Hope of the World*: Protestant Pedagogy and the Visual Culture of the London Missionary Society', in *Material Religion: The Journal of Objects, Art and Belief*, Issue 1, March 2005)

Carpenter, H & Prichard, M (1984) *The Oxford Companion to Children's Literature*, Oxford: University Press

Cutt, M N (1974) *Mrs Sherwood and her Books for Children*, Oxford: University Press

Day, K B (1999) *A.L.O.E.: Writing Home*, Unpublished MA dissertation, University of Roehampton

Day, K B (2001) 'A.L.O.E.: Between Two Worlds' in Pinsent, P (ed.) *The Big Issues: Representations of Socially Marginalized Groups and Individuals in Children's Literature, Past and Present*, Roehampton: National Centre for Research in Children's Literature Papers 6.

Ferguson, N (2003) *Empire: How Britain made the Modern World*, London: Allen Lane (Penguin Press)

James, L (1997) Raj: *The Making and Unmaking of British India*, London: Little, Brown & Co.

McCrum, R, Mcran, W & MacNeil, R (1986) *The Story of English*, London: Faber

Smith, N R (1946) *The State of Mind of Mrs Sherwood*, London: Macmillan

Said, E (1985) *Orientalism*, Harmondsworth: Penguin

Said, E (1993) *Culture and Imperialism*, London: Chatto and Windus

Part 2

Middle and Far East

The History of Children's Literature in Iran

Taraneh Matloob

A greater understanding of literature and its role in the lives of children within a culture can be acquired by studying both the history of childhood and the history of children's literature. Identifying images of childhood as revealed in culture and society over time offers clear evidence of children's status in Iranian society, illustrating such aspects as: when Iranian society started considering children as different from adults; how thinkers have defined the child and the special needs of children; when children's literature began; and the historical period in which the first books were produced in Iran.

From the study of historical resources, it appears that the concept of childhood in the area concerned goes as far back as far as three thousand years ago. The analysis of oral literature, myths, old Zorastrian documents, illustrations, and manuscripts reflects the life of Iranian children in different periods. Some objects dating to ancient times address different aspects of childhood in Iran; many images of children's lives are depicted on archaeological artifacts. These include the image of a mother giving a bird to her child as a toy, engraved on an Achaemenid seal, and a terracotta bust of a mother holding a child in her arms.

Figure 1: 'Woman giving a bird to her daughter", relief on a ring, Achaemenid period, 500-300 B.C
© Institute of Research on the history of Children's Literature in Iran 2003

Research in post-Islamic works also makes it clear that there are texts and illustrations that are directly or indirectly addressed to children. An illustrated version of GhaaboosNaameh showing pupils studying in old-fashioned primary schools (MaktabKhanehs) and images of children in old miniatures are examples of this.

Figure 2: Traditional schools in Islamic period paintings
© *Institute of Research on the history of Children's Literature in Iran 2003*

In documents from the Islamic era, the views of the philosopher Avecenna about raising children are notable. In an invaluable thousand-year-old document about lullabies, Avecenna says that for the proper nurturing of healthy newborn children, two things besides feeding are essential: one is gently rocking the baby and the other is regularly singing a soft lullaby to put the child to sleep. The more children are rocked and hear music the more they will develop physically and mentally.

Figure 3: Abou-Ali-sina (980-1036), Avicenna, one of the greatest physicians of the middle Ages and an outstanding philosopher. He developed important theories on child psychology.
© Institute of Research on the history of Children's Literature in Iran 2003

The History of Children's Literature in Iran (HCLI) is a research project undertaken by the Institute for Research on the History of Children's Literature in Iran (IRHCLI). Started in 1997, the project is planned to be spread over 10 volumes. The first six of these volumes have already been published and work continues on the remaining ones. The HCLI project includes such issues as the first appearance of culture and literature in the area concerned, and the formation of oral literature and its components, followed by the appearance of children's literature in ancient times. It goes on to include the era after the advent of Islam, the early part of the twentieth century, and the development of children's literature up to the Islamic Revolution in 1979.

Research in pre-Islamic and Islamic works makes it clear that there are very few texts addressed directly to children. However, many passages can be found in the general literary works that are written for children and are clearly addressed to the young reader. This has been discussed extensively in volumes 1 and 2 of the HCLI.

Figure 4: Shangool va Mangool, an old Iranian folktale for children, lithography.
© *Institute of Research on the history of Children's Literature in Iran 2003*

The turning point occurs in the late nineteenth and early twentieth century, when additional factors enter the scene, such as new educational concepts. Other aspects discussed in these volumes include the continuity of oral literature and folklore, the development of simpler Persian prose, the advent of translations from the West, the start of the printing industry in Iran, establishment of new schools, the study of child psychology, and the rise of pioneering personalities as early publishers of books for children.

In this project, the broader socio-economic and cultural situations will also be reviewed in light of historical developments. Sample text illustrations from the different periods will complete the discussions and provide a unique anthology. As an extensive research project, the HCLI will also review the children's literature of Iran's minorities such as the Azaris, the Kurds, Zorastrians, Christians and Jews. More information can be found on the website: http://www.chlhistory.org

The Representation of Arabs in Children's Literature

Ann Lazim

My interest in how Arabs are represented in children's literature dates back to the1970s when I met my husband, who is Iraqi. As part of my studies in children's librarianship I was asked to compile a booklist on a topic of my choosing and I decided that to make the Arab world the subject of this would help me discover more about my husband's region of origin. Since that time I have taken an active interest in the portrayal of Arab characters in children's books, seeking relevant material, both positive and negative. This has led to my researching this subject for my MA dissertation. The thoughts below refer to work in progress, and mainly relate to some recent children's fiction.

Fiction featuring Arabs was difficult to find in the 1970s, particularly stories with contemporary settings. There were some historical novels and, as now, retellings and variants of *The Arabian Nights*. During the 1970s and 1980s, there was an increasing awareness among librarians, teachers and parents about racist stereotyping and the absence of various cultural groups from British children's literature[1]. Attention at that stage focused on the most visible ethnic minority communities in the UK, mainly those from Africa, the Caribbean and Asia (specifically India, Pakistan and Bangladesh). Arabs were a hidden community as far as British children's literature was concerned.

This is still largely the case, although as a result of the global situation interest is growing. Increasingly, adults, especially teachers, are asking for books set in or about the Middle East, to share with and recommend to children. A few recent novels feature well-rounded and interesting Arab characters. *A Little Piece of Ground* (2003), by Elizabeth Laird and Sonia Nimr, is set in occupied Palestine; daily life is seen through the eyes of twelve-year-old Karim as he and his friends try to lead a normal life by claiming a piece of ground where they can play football in peace. The humiliations the Palestinians suffer are made explicit and this has led some critics to suggest that the book should have also indicated that not all Israelis agree with the oppression of the Palestinians[2]. However, this book was written to portray what life is actually like on a day-to-day basis for Karim and many others like him and, sadly, their experiences rarely include contact with Israeli peacemakers.

Linda Newbery is a writer whose books frequently portray war and its legacy, and her recent novel, *Sisterland* (2004), includes this aspect among its variety of themes. Reviewers have emphasised the discovery by the main character, Hilly, of her Jewish ancestry, and her grandmother's Alzheimer's disease. However, a significant strand in the novel is the developing relationship between Hilly and Rashid, a young Palestinian man. When Hilly decides to visit Israel to seek out relatives, the two young people have a very forthright conversation that gives clear insight into Rashid's position and why he finds her decision difficult to accept:

> 'You had Jewish relatives in Germany but that was then, and this is now. You don't have to turn into a Zionist sympathizer! And you will, if you go out there. They'll tell you Israel's got a sacred right to their Promised Land, and the Arabs are a fanatical band of killers. Hilly, I've just come back from there! Israel's the enemy. I hate them. I don't want to, don't want to hate, but I can't tell you how much I hate them. Can you begin to imagine what it's like to live under occupation? Curfews, road blocks, rules telling you where you can and can't go? Soldiers killed my cousin, killed him in the street! Can't you see where that puts us? It's like, it's like – I can't even think of another example – no, it's like I tell you my grandad was an SS Kommandant or something. Only this is happening *now*.' (2004: 344)

Whatever their own political views, readers cannot fail to be moved by the passion conveyed in this outburst, particularly since it is spoken by a character with whom both the reader and the central character are empathetic. Especially notable is the repetition of key words such as 'hate' and 'killed', together with the powerful simile in the penultimate sentence. Earlier in their relationship, Rashid has talked to Hilly about the West Bank, the Occupied Territories; about Israeli roadblocks, tanks in the streets, curfews and restrictions. He talked about the massacre at the Jenin refugee camp, of houses bulldozed, helicopters firing on civilians, people bleeding to death while the Israeli soldiers refused to let ambulances near; of the rage that turned young Palestinians into suicide bombers. (2004: 268)

This catalogue of horrific events, almost unimaginable to young readers in Britain, has a powerful visual quality, adding to the emotive effect of the passage.

There has been a well-established tradition of books for young people describing the horrors perpetrated against Jews in Europe during World War Two. The memories of those atrocities have made many Europeans reluctant to criticise Israel for the crimes now being committed against the Palestinians. It is rare to find a book like *Sisterland* which attempts to make these necessary historical links for a young audience. Newbery's novel also provides a challenge to other stereotyped assumptions, since Hilly's best friend Reuben is in a gay relationship with Rashid's brother, Saeed. However, the young people shield the Palestinian boy's parents from knowledge about this situation, realising that their cultural background would probably make it difficult for them to accept their son's homosexuality.

The few books with contemporary settings that do portray Arab characters mainly concentrate on the Palestine/Israel situation. A recent article in *The Horn Book Magazine* by Elsa Marston (2004) focuses on this part of the Arab world, describing a number of novels and picture books, most of which were originally published in the USA, although Elizabeth Laird's *A Little Piece of Ground* (which, as Marston observes, has not been published at all in the USA) and *Dreaming of Palestine* (2003) by Randa Ghazy, which was first published in Italy, are also included.

The war in Iraq and the ongoing occupation have not as yet led to much literature for children and young people, at least not with a direct setting in the region. However, many authors and illustrators contributed to an anti-war anthology *Lines in the Sand* (2003), edited by Mary Hoffman and Rhiannon Lassiter, inspired by strong feelings about the war in Iraq. Although a few of the stories and excerpts in this collection, such as 'Mr Shaabi' by Pnina Kass and 'Heads on the Pillow' by Alan Gibbons, include Arab characters, the poems and most of the stories tend to look at the horrors of war in a more universalised way. An excerpt from Kevin Crossley-Holland's *King of the Middle March* (also looked at later in my article) provides a context for conflict by recalling the Crusades, while Elizabeth Laird contributes a short extract from her journal about a visit to the Marsh Arabs, emphasising the warmth of Arab hospitality.

Some novelists have very effectively enabled readers to share the feelings of characters involved in conflicts. Robert Westall's impressive novel *Gulf* (1992), set at the time of the earlier Gulf War in Kuwait, gives moving insight into the feelings of an Iraqi boy soldier. This is filtered through the body and mind of an English boy who appears to have in some mysterious way exchanged places with him and entered his consciousness. More recently, Julia Jarman's *The Peace Weavers* (2004) portrays the mother of the main protagonist as having gone to Iraq to be part of a 'human shield'.

In addition to books which deal with the conflicts in the Arab World, it is essential for readers to have the opportunity to encounter non-stereotypical Arab characters in a more normal, everyday-life, situation. *Benny and Omar* (1998), by Eoin Colfer, set in Tunisia, is a humorous story about friendship between an Irish boy and a Tunisian boy, although there is sadness in Omar's life. The boys find ways to communicate using slogans from advertising, TV and films:

> 'Where's your family, Omar?' asked Benny. Then he tried to convert it to television-speak. 'Ah… Homer Simpson?'
>
> Omar nodded. '*Doh!*' he said, slapping his forehead.
> 'Okay… You Bart. Homer and Marge?'

The Tunisian boy computed this. 'No Homer. No Marge.'
He looked suddenly sad. Benny was sorry he'd asked. Omar pointed down towards the railway crossing. A triangle of green lights was the only illumination on Gabes Road.

He took a long breath. 'Homer. Marge: Thomas the Tank Engine – boom.'

Benny swallowed. Being Tunisian wasn't easy. Having a moped suddenly didn't seem like all that much of a plus. Benny didn't know what to say. And even if he had, he couldn't have translated it.

'Lisa,' said Omar.

'Huh?'

'Homer, Marge – boom. Lisa: Casualty, Chicago Hope.' (1998: 83)

The commonplace, even banal, use of television programmes as a medium of communication contributes a greater degree of pathos to Omar's situation, while revealing the commonality of interests between the two boys.

In recent historical novels, the revival of interest in the Crusades surely is more than coincidental within the current belligerent political climate. Catherine Jinks' *Pagan's Crusade* was first published in 1992, close to the time of the Gulf War, and was reissued in 2003. Events set in and around Jerusalem in 1187 are related in short staccato sentences in a humorous tone by a young squire. References to the 'infidel' are much fewer than in G A Henty's nineteenth century adventure *Winning His Spurs A Tale of the Crusades* (1882), the story of Cuthbert, a young hero and willing recruit to the Crusades who becomes a knight at a very young age; in the older book there are frequent references to 'wresting the holy sepulchre from the infidel.' However, such allusions are certainly still there in the recent novel, as in this passage:

Sudden uproar from the nearest knot of defenders. Spin around and God! An Infidel! Bright blood – open mouth – flashing sword – screaming and screaming...

He disappears in a thrashing tangle of bodies. Hasn't a hope. Hasn't a hope. But there's another one. Rising over the heads – look out!

'Look out!'

A blade jabs out of that boiling mess. Straight into the Infidel's stomach. He drops like a stone... reeling back into empty air ... disappearing ... But the next one takes his place. (2003: 190-1)

The abrupt staccato phrases create an element of danger and tension, but there appears to be little concern about the humanity of the protagonist's opponents.

A much more thoughtful approach is evident in both *Blood Red Horse* (2004) by K M Grant and in *Arthur: King of the Middle March* (2003) by Kevin Crossley-Holland, although the latter writer is much more searching in his questioning about the 'necessity' for the crusades. The book's press release indicates that the author 'has been inevitably influenced by world events, as obvious comparisons have cropped up between the current political climate and that of Arthur's world.' The excerpt, previously mentioned, in *Lines in the Sand,* entitled 'Jihad', reveals the mutual incomprehension between the warring forces about unfamiliar customs, while making clear that cruelty towards the Saracen women is a habitual event within this warring situation, to the horror of the protagonist.

The genre of fantasy repays deeper investigation within the context of the portrayal of Arab characters. Intertextual use of *The Arabian Nights* is common in many fantasies, though it is not always employed sensitively. For example, in *Children of the Lamp* (2004) by P B Kerr, the central characters, twins John and Philippa, discover they are djinn. To aid them in realizing this, their uncle Nimrod encourages them to read *The Arabian Nights.* In Kerr's highly hyped novel, described by Nicholas Tucker as 'An arch, patronising, xenophobic yarn' (*The Independent*, 29/11/04), names are often used and cultural references made, in a manner which recalls the Orientalism so rife in the books examined by Edward Said (1978). The names used for the Egyptian characters have racist overtones and pay more attention to their potential for humour than to any more authentic identity. 'Baksheesh' immediately suggests begging, while 'Huamai' and 'Toeragh' rely on phonetic wordplay. The use of 'Creemy' as a nickname for Karim recalls the way in which so many Western people seem to be reluctant to bother to use the real names of foreigners. Throughout my reading of this book, I found myself recalling John Stephens' discussion of a much more subtle text, *Castle in the Air* by Diana Wynne Jones: 'the larger world-context influences the state of the text' (1992: 278)

Accompanying the need for accurate representation of Arab characters in children's fiction, is that for the provision for English-speaking readers of children's books by authors and illustrators of Arab origin. Such books and authors are hard to find. One exception is Arab-American Naomi Shihab Nye, whose picture book *Sitti's Secrets* (1994) was published in the UK by Hamish Hamilton but did not make it to paperback before vanishing. Her poetry and her novel *Habibi* (1997) have never been published in Britain. There is also Rafik Schami, a Syrian writing in German, whose novel *A Handful of Stars* (1990), set in Damascus, was published in English but is now out of print. While it is understandable that publishers may be reluctant to publish, or to retain in print, books which have not sold well, it is surely incumbent on them, and on all involved in the world of children's literature, to give more attention to books which, by increasing knowledge of and empathy with unfamiliar cultures, can be agents in reducing the hostility which all too often arises from fear of the unknown.

Notes

1. See, for example: Bob Dixon (1977) *Catching Them Young*. Vol.I *Sex Race and Class in Children's Fiction*. Vol.2 *Political Ideas in Children's Fiction*, London: Pluto Press; Gillian Klein (1985) *Reading into Racism*, London: Routledge and Kegan Paul; Pat Pinsent, *Children's Literature and the Politics of Equality*, David Fulton Publishers, 1997.

2. See `Children's author faces Jewish wrath' in *The Guardian* 23/8/03, and Elizabeth Laird, 'How the authors of Children's Books Perceive their Audiences,' in (ed.) P Pinsent, *Books and Boundaries*, pp14-18, Pied Piper Publishing, 2004

Bibliography

Primary Texts

Colfer, E (1998) *Benny and Omar,* Dublin: O'Brien Press

Crossley-Holland, K (2003) *Arthur: King of the Middle March,* London: Orion

Ghazy, R (2003) *Dreaming of Palestine*, translated by Marguerite Shore, George Braziller Publisher, New York

Grant, K M (2004) *Blood Red Horse,* London: Puffin

Henty, G A (n.d.; first published 1882) *Winning His Spurs. A Tale of the Crusades,* London: Sampson Low, Marston & Co.

Jarman, J (2004) *The Peace Weavers,* London: Andersen Press

Jinks, C (2003) *Pagan's Crusade,* London: Collins

Kerr, P B (2004) *Children of the Lamp: The Akhenaten Adventure*, London: Scholastic

Laird, E & Nimr, S (2003) *A Little Piece of Ground,* London: Macmillan

Newbery, L (2004) *Sisterland,* London: Red Fox

Nye, N S (1997) *Habibi,* New York: Simon & Schuster

Nye, N S & Carpenter, N (1994) *Sitti's Secrets,* London: Hamish Hamilton

Schami, R (1990) *A Handful of Stars*, translated by Rika Lesser, London: Gollancz

Westall, R (1992) *Gulf,* London: Methuen

Secondary Texts

Marston, E (2004) 'A Window in the Wall: Palestinians in Children's Literature' in *The Horn Book Magazine*, November/December 2004, pp647-655

Said, E W (2003; first published 1978) *Orientalism,* London: Penguin

Stephens, J (1992) *Language and Ideology in Children's Fiction*, Harlow, Essex: Longman

Children's Paradise: Texts and Pictures for Young Audiences in China between 1918 and 1947

Marian Allsobrook

Children's Paradise is the title of one of the numerous supplements and magazines published for children in China in the twentieth century. The title is used here both positively and ironically, since the period from 1918 to the mid-twentieth-century is marked by a double flowering of output for young readers, first in the years before the 1937 invasion by Japan and again in the fifties. The concept of children's literature as a garden frequently appears in the imagery used by critics and editors during this period. Mary Ann Farquhar (1999) notes the pastoral images of Chinese children's literature in the early twentieth century as a garden of hope and delight, emancipating children from the dark night of Confucian orthodoxy. She notes that although both Confucian and May Fourth (see below) views on education share a recognition of the social importance of the educative role of children's books, the latter, seeking to shape China's future, pursued an interest in Western child psychology and the nature of childhood, which undermined Confucian educational practice.[1]

Intellectual debate about children's imaginative and social needs as future citizens accompanied the publication of plays, poems, songs, stories and pictorial narratives, or comic books, for an enormous audience. However, although idealised childhoods do feature in some texts, existence for most of the young characters portrayed is far removed from paradise. One of the most influential writers and editors of children's texts, Ye Shengtao (1894-1988), portrays the poverty and misery which afflicted children; in his short stories he urges active participation by young people in the rebuilding of Chinese society.

In a very different genre, that of the comic book or pictorial narrative, the story of a street child, Sanmao, first created by Zhang Leping in 1935, became so potent that fiction and reality blurred in people's minds: children wrote letters offering Sanmao a home. He became so popular that four discrete versions of the orphan's life were produced. Sanmao came into existence as a strip cartoon character and representative of an oppressed class; his name was used as the title of a comic and the 1947 version of Sanmao, *An Orphan on the Streets*, became a classic.

I have chosen some of Ye Shengtao's stories and Zhang Leping's Sanmao to represent important developments in Chinese children's literature during the first half of the twentieth century. They reflect the history of those decades and the desire to engage an audience which previously had been reared on traditional texts and Confucian principles. Dorothea Hayward Scott

(1980: 130-134) discusses the ways in which the fortunes of the publishing houses, particularly those in Shanghai, reflected the century's turbulent events.

Ye Shengtao did much to promote the use of the vernacular; he was intent on establishing a canon of Chinese children s literature and like many others was active in the New Culture Movement, or May Fourth movement, which began in 1918 as a response to the ceding of territories in China, perceived by Chinese reformers as betrayal. There has been a recent revival of academic interest in this movement and its principles by scholars such as Lijun Bi, who cites as an example a recent poem 'It is Children's Day Today,' which validates a shared humanity. The arms industry, gambling and corruption are condemned in the poem as destructive of global harmony and future survival. The recent revival of interest encourages us to re-consider the response of Ye Shengtao and others to Western texts for children by Oscar Wilde and Hans Christian Andersen. By so doing, we can inform ourselves about the surge of editorial, literary and artistic activity for children in China during the first half of the twentieth century.

The growth of interest in the special nature of childhood and the influence of Verne, Gorky and John Dewey[2] at the start of the twentieth century in China, are areas of great significance, but beyond the range of this study; such concepts and such thinkers allowed Chinese writers to distance themselves from Confucian tradition in their desire to use the vernacular for the new writing. There was an urgent need for scientific education in China, and for reform of the complex hierarchical structures which the examination system underpinned. These factors stimulated translations of Verne's work. Gorky's tales came to be regarded as a model for children's literature from the mid-nineteen-thirties, after he became a major spokesman on new Soviet children's literature.

Ye Shengtao sought to explain society in a way that a young audience could understand, interpreting power structures in 'The Emperor's New Clothes.' In *The Language of Birds and Animals*, using creatures as characters, he depicts a society ravaged by military aggression, questioning the rhetoric of war. Graphic details such as the bomber's dark shadow flying overhead and the orator's mouth like that of a rhinoceros suggest that aggression is an unjustifiable cause of suffering, and evidence of human self-importance.

From the two short story collections for children by Shengtao, the title story of one, *The Scarecrow* (1923) depicts a main character whose immobility limits his potential. He is a powerless observer of human despair and imminent famine. Guarding a crop night and day, he watches a plague of insects which he is unable to deal with. During the night a starving woman with a sick child arouses intense pity in the scarecrow. Another woman drowns herself rather than endure her husband's abuse. The principle of helping others is strongly predicated in the story, drawing upon Confucian concepts of filial devotion. The child reader would hear the urgency and absorb the figurative call for action, as the scarecrow urges the day to dawn and the birds to fly. Only then will the peasants be alerted to the threat that the insects represent. In the title story of his second collection, *The Statue of the Ancient Hero* (1931), Ye Shengtao questions the notion of heroic status as a construct: a statue assumes superiority over the smaller stone fragments that provide a pedestal and base. All came from the same block and eventually both statue and base are crushed to serve as road-building material. The story was published in the first issue of the magazine *The Juvenile Student*, in which the editorial commented upon the rich satire of Ye Shengtao's stories. Like the scarecrow, the statue is given an intense inner life - here of vanity - because he inspires the masses to work with fresh energy. He even disparages the Buddha by comparison with himself as a figure of inspiration. 'Success comes to those who work hard,' the narrator says early in the narrative, but the adulation enjoyed by the statue is the result of the sculptor's talent and the statue himself has in no way earned the praise. The stone chips at his feet remind him of their shared origin and of their role in supporting him as a statue. Ye Shengtao establishes the tensions between a figurehead and the masses. He suggests that myth and reality can blur, distorting the truth; citizens are as likely to worship nonentities as genuine heroes. During the night the statue falls and shatters; his identity is completely lost.

The Hans Christian Andersen story of the emperor's new clothes was appropriated by Ye Shengtao during the New Culture Movement. Whereas in Andersen's story the innocent child identifies the emperor's self-delusion, in Ye Shengtao's story, which takes the narrative further, the ludic elements are stressed from the first page and robust mockery from the crowd is used for dialogue. Heightening the absurdity in this way, Ye Shengtao prepares for bold contrast when the emperor retaliates brutally with sentences of death. Imperial concubines and ministers suffer despite their attempts at discretion, and mass executions continue, until the people exploit their numbers and accost the emperor directly, intimidating him. Naked, grimacing, he is a ridiculous figure, compared with a monkey stung by hornets and a bruised chicken caught out in the rain. The emperor, completely stripped of his authority, falls unconscious to the ground. Instead of the clear-sighted child, it is the people who confront the emperor and diminish him.

A later story, 'The Experiences of a Locomotive' (1936), was first published in a new magazine called *The New Adolescents*, which Ye Shengtao edited with others. The urgency of this story on the eve of the Japanese invasion of China calls for military activism. The mood is very different from that of 'The Scarecrow', with its anguished main character. Active participation is needed to secure equality. The locomotive demonstrates the virtues of united response, dedication and selflessness. He is another protagonist given life by the author to struggle against oppressive hierarchical factions.

It is possible here to suggest only some of the early twentieth century influences which combined to achieve a potent body of politicised writing in China for children, writing in which the anguish of the poor is set against the potential might of their numbers. Mary Ann Farquhar (1999) identifies a new sensibility in Ye Shengtao, who was writing at a time when a vernacular urban literature was developing and the memorising of classical Confucian scripts was yielding to a more modern curriculum. In 'The Scarecrow,' Ye Shengtao's inanimate protagonist is endowed with humane intensity of feeling, despite his physical immobility, while compassion for those caught up in the carnage of war is discussed in *The Language of Birds and Animals*. In both 'The Experiences of a Locomotive' and 'The Statue of the Ancient Hero,' the collective responses respectively of the zealous students, and of the stone chips slighted by the grand statue they support, express the power of a united vision for reform.

What had started as a preoccupation with the special nature of childhood and the child's consciousness shifted to a collective endeavour to harness the invincible masses of the future. In 1928, the story ‘Only One Hand’, published by Guo Moruo under an assumed name, portrays a heroic fifteen year old worker in a Shanghai factory. Farquhar outlines the thinly disguised exposure of factory conditions: when his sleeve catches in machinery, the young worker loses a hand. Using the severed hand like a weapon, he knocks away the gun brandished by the factory boss. Moruo compares him to a wounded lion (Farquhar 1999: 151).The narrative draws upon real-life experience of factory conditions and calls for unity in the workers' movement.

It was during this decade that Mao Zedong was gaining power. One aspect of this was the establishing of a rural base in Yan'an. Before this, much of the debate and development of ideas had been concentrated in Shanghai and Beijing, indeed, the bulk of the audience for children's literature was urban. By 1937, children's literature was mobilised as part of China's war effort targeting Shanghai, where the publishing industry was based, and the rural areas. Writers now consciously sought the rural masses as their audience: Farquhar argues that the war had a dramatic impact on Chinese children's literature. In particular, the portrayal of the militant hero, a youngster who might courageously fight both the Japanese and the treacherous Chinese, represented the peasant classes, in rapid action and bold characterisation.

Jane Parish Yang considers the communist ideology which subsumed the interests of the individual and the family in favour of society as a whole. Struggling to accommodate such directives, writers' naturalistic tendencies were at odds with the desired portrayal of exemplary characters only. She comments on the tendency of writers after the Communist victory in 1949 not to portray negative characters who were vacillating or too individualistic, but instead favouring positive role models who served their community and society. She argues that the more naturalistic characterisation which had existed before this point was managed only under pressure to prioritise the collective good of society (1998: 87-89).

The ideological function of writing for Chinese children shapes the creativity of the authors and artists considered here; it gathered strength as the twentieth century advanced. In 1938, the Federation of Writers and Artists expressed its sense of patriotic urgency in the first edition of its magazine, *Literature of the War of Resistance*, stating that the true artworker must forcefully use the weapon of Art; he 'must express Society realistically and he must reinforce this with his own work of motivating that Society.' Farquhar quotes from the first edition of the federation's magazine: 'Art is an expression of Society; it is also a driving force in Society.' Children's writers were now firmly included with 'art-workers' and shared a similar social mission (1999: 172). There were war stories such as 'The Little Traitor' by Su Su (1940), which portrays a boy tricked into spying for traitors, who is redeemed by heroic action. Su Su was one of the major contributing editors to the Juvenile Publishing House, which had started by producing small pamphlet-magazines for children, as part of the patriotic effort. A measure of the publishing activity for child readers is indicated in the discussion of the titles *Good Children*, (which changed its name to *Reading for Children*) and 'The Juvenile Publishing House' which established a readership of poems, plays, stories and translations for children. Proscription on publication and closure came in 1941 (Farquhar 1999: 169-171).

Mao Zedong's famous 'Talks at the Yan'an Forum on Literature and Art' in 1942 sought to merge literature (including children's literature) with the war effort. Farquhar sees Mao's Talks in 1942 as crystallising certain trends in revolutionary literary theory in the pre-war period, setting guidelines for the later organisation of the publishing industry in China, including comics (1999: 192-198). One effect of the guidelines set out in his text was that art and literature were now seen as ideological weapons; the impact of both text and pictorial narrative was recognised and articulated. Work had to be accessible and attractive. Traditional art forms, which ordinary people could understand, were cited as examples of what was needed. The history of pictorial narrative in China reaches back a thousand years, and the popularisation of the picture book as a revolutionary cultural product was a significant contribution to the development of Chinese children's literature. Street opera offers another visual contribution: its characters and stories frequently found their way into the comic book.

Mao Dun had claimed in 1932 that the comic book, if utilised cleverly, could certainly become the most powerful work in mass literature and art. He wrote of the rapid rise in reading ability in Shanghai and of the inadequacy of reading materials to satisfy primary school children. Rented comic books could be read on the spot. For Mao Dun these bookstalls 'have become the most powerful and popular tool for mass education.' (Farquhar 1999: 196-198).Very often prominent artists created the pictures and the comic book was discussed in critical articles. Mao Dun's children's story *Big Nose* (1936) features a character who loves street stall comic books, especially those in which women sword fighters appear.

A black and white photo of a street stall renting out comic books was the picture chosen for the cover of the commemorative publication of comic book art illustrations issued by the Hong Kong Heritage Museum to mark their inaugural exhibition, 'Hong Kong Comic World' in 2000. In this publication, an example of Sanmao is included. The cover shows three children avidly studying a rented comic book; behind them the books available for hire on the street are pegged up. That this was the area of cultural interest chosen for the first exhibition by the museum indicates the measure of significance attributed to comic books. Zhang Leping's versions of Sanmao became the most famous examples of comic books; the 1947 *An Orphan on the Streets* opens with the child's realisation that creatures are nurtured by their parents while he has to fend for himself. The opening frames show Sanmao in his primary role. as observer; four examples of parental nurturing among creatures remind him of his own neglected circumstances. When he attempts to hug one puppy in a litter, he is chased by its snarling mother up a tree. All his subsequent chances of joining a kindly family are doomed. Very often his generous attempts to help others are not appreciated; most humans are depicted as callous and brutal.

Dreams are a consistent and traditional feature in Chinese literature, here used by Zhang Leping to great effect. The device by which Sanmao is roused to reality consistently adds humour to the narrative. Zhang Leping uses sense impressions which begin within the dream, only to undergo an alarming change. which alerts him to his real predicament (p61). Sanmao's dreams give the reader insight into his inner life: obviously he dreams about food, but sleeping in the cupboard under the stairs - like Harry Potter- he also dreams of the luxury of receiving a gift. This turns out to be a fur coat, which, as he unwraps it, turns into a snarling tiger. Sanmao wakes to find a snapping cat on his chest. Very often his dreams shift alarmingly in this way as he is brought back to an unwelcome reality. Dreaming of having a loving mother, who then cries to see the cuts and bruises on his back, he wakes to discover the water drops are in fact rain soaking him on the balcony where he has tried to sleep.

Later, imprisoned, he dreams of escape into a normal, happy childhood where cleanliness, education, friendship and play are enjoyed; reality for him is a perpetual gamble of quick-witted opportunism. Exploited by a street performer, he becomes an unwilling contortionist; these experiences are depicted with much humour. Coming across a baby abandoned, he endeavours to find it a home, but the life of the street offers no easy comfort.

Most of the frames are set four to a page, but there are some large, single illustrations filling the whole page. One of these, at the end, shows Sanmao refusing American weapons; the American is dressed as Father Christmas. The final frame reveals a scene of street violence, as humanity is consumed by hatred and conflict. Sanmao stands, a tiny central figure, disillusioned and alone, taking in the scene, which is largely constructed of frames within the artist's full page space. Entrances, windows and vehicle doors, even roof-top spaces, provide vignettes of corruption, despair, indifference and aggression. A pet is saved, but a tiny child lies howling in the gutter (p155). Zhang Leping's art conveys the energy of street life, the moment by moment sharpness of the orphan's responses and his crucial role as observer of human nature. Very often he is looking through a window, or at a shop front, a cinema screen, a poster, or in his imagination picturing alternatives to his street existence. As the reader of the pictorial narrative has to make sense of what he looks at, so the little hero has continually to make sense of what he observes, if he is to survive.

Farquhar (1999: 207) notes that Zhang Leping was friendly with some of the street orphans of Shanghai; what he observed motivated him to create the fictional symbol of Sanmao. She refers to the hundreds of thousands of orphaned street children in Shanghai before 1949 and includes comments from the playwright Ria Yan in 1950, who wrote of the character Sanmao as so much loved: 'not an abstract creation of the artist's brush but a real flesh-and-blood child of misery who incites pity and love' (1999: 207-210). Whereas the enemy had been the Japanese invaders, now the enemy is the indifferent, corrupt elite. The bold contrasts of the needy and the privileged, the generous and the brutal, the longed-for ideal, or children's paradise, and the stark reality also suggest that the new Communist China is represented by Sanmao's dreams of a fulfilled childhood and the old China by oppression and poverty. Apart from the dramatic contrasts established, the narrative gains impact from its humorous suggestion of Sanmao's well-meaning efforts: his babycare, food preparation and stove lighting, and his agonised contortions when coerced into street performance, are consistently entertaining. A graphic portrayal of everyday life is recorded within the narrative frames.

The writer Ye Shengtao looked to the west for literary models and adapted what he used to a specific Marxist content, which proved to be influential within China. His stories 'The Scarecrow' and 'The Statue of the Ancient Hero' were both selected as exemplary models for other writers to emulate during the Maoist period. Zhang Leping's artistry and vision created an enduring fictional character in Sanmao, whose experience evokes the harsh reality of street children's existence across the world today.

The strongly visual impact of Ye Shengtao's stories (which were accompanied by woodcuts) and the haunting pictorial portrayal of the street child Sanmao should properly be considered within the spectacular cultural wealth of China's artistic and narrative tradition which awaits the full engagement of western scholars. The stories which have received attention here express the intensity of the struggle for survival and reform, yet the vision of a secure childhood, nurturing all the potential that a young person might possess, is present within the frames of *An Orphan on the Streets.* It is echoed in the pictorial narrative created by the artist Lo Koon Chiu, published in 1963 in *Children's Paradise Bi-monthly*, which the Hong Kong Museum of Art displayed in 2004. Lo Koon Chiu's drawings express the reflective pleasures of childhood as well as the active pursuits of playground games. For Sanmao, the comfort of meals, clean showers, education, friendship and parental affection feature in an alluring dream he has while in prison. The reality of street life is very different from the children's paradise his imagination conjures up.

Notes

1. See also Farquhar (1999: 92) on the Romantic trend in May Fourth literature, and the return to nature.

2. The influence of Dewey, Gorky and Verne are discussed by Farquhar (1999: 30, & 45-51)

Bibliography

Farquhar, Mary Ann (1999) *Children's Literature in China*, New York and London: M E Sharpe Armonk

Lijun Bi (2003) 'Capitalist Bears and Social Modernisation: Chinese Children's Literature in the Post-Mao Period' in *Children's Literature in Education*, vol. 34, no. l, March 2003, pp57-73.

Scott, Dorothea Hayward (1980) *Chinese Popular Literature and the Child*, Chicago: American Library Association

Yang, Jane Parish (1998) ‘A Change in the Family: The Image of the Family in Contemporary Chinese Children's Literature, 19491993,’ in *Children's Literature* 26

Ye Shengtao (1949) *The Scarecrow* and *The Statue of the Ancient Hero*, Shanghai: K'ai-ming Book Co.

Zhang Leping (1988) *An Orphan on the Streets*, Hong Kong: Joint Publishing Company (HK) Ltd.

Breaking Away from Mickey Mouse: Children's Literature in Laos and across the Globe

How and why does a separate written children's literature emerge in any given language or culture? Are there common patterns of development? What is the relationship between the development of literacy and an indigenous children's literature? What has been the role of invasion and colonisation in determining the form, content and purpose of children's literature? These were some of the overarching questions that have provided a starting point for this discussion.

1. Encouraging Indigenous Children's Literature in Laos

Yukie Ito

The initial focus of this discussion is the activities of the None Government Organisation (NGO) called Deknoylao (Action with Lao Children). It was first established in 1982 in Tokyo by a Lao woman, Chanthasong Inthavong, as the 'Association for Sending Picture Books to Lao Children of Japan (ASPB)'. Since then, it has been working mainly on children's book production in Laos. I myself came to be engaged in the NGO as a volunteer, and have learned a great deal from other volunteers and paid staff, and from my practical involvement in its activities. In this paper, I will first give some background information about Laos itself and the situation of children's books there. Then I will explain the activities of our NGO, which is encouraging indigenous children's literature in Laos.

Literacy and children's books in Laos

Laos is often called 'the last Shangri-La in Asia', suggesting that it is still an unknown country to many people. Located between Thailand and Vietnam, it is a socialist country characterised by multi-ethnicity, with an estimated 68 ethnic minority groups. Many traces remain from the period when it was colonised by France, but subsequently the country has been greatly influenced by Thailand, both culturally and economically. Many products are imported from Thailand, including Thai TV dramas and popular songs. As a consequence, many young Laotians can speak Thai, a language fairly similar to Lao. A culture of reading and writing has not yet developed in Laos, because the country has the heritage of an oral culture, while the lengthy colonial period hindered dissemination of reading and writing of the Lao language. In addition, little interest has been shown in books except for practical reasons. Even today, few children's books are written in Lao, and many books found in Laos are from Thailand. During 1999, for instance, publications in the Lao language numbered only 57 books for general readers, 3 magazines, 22 children's books, and 20 text books (figures from Deknoylao NGO).

The shortage of books has led to relatively low literacy rates. According to the UNESCO Institute for Statistics (UIS) the male literacy rate in Laos was 77.4 percent, while that for women was 55.5 percent[1]. There is evidence that some people actually lose their ability to read and write after they graduate from school, since there are few opportunities to come into contact with written materials. Also, these data refer only to the literacy rate of people over 15 years old. Children are regarded as literate, because they are supposed to be learning to read or write in schools. However, some children drop out of school for family or economic reasons, and thus do not become fully literate.

Members of Deknoylao believe that the ability to read and write is essential for a fully active role in modern society, since access to information is so important. Although the country has a rich oral tradition, it will be unable to compete in the modern world if its population remains largely illiterate. The problem is exacerbated by the fact that many of the estimated 68 ethnic minority groups have their own languages. The official language, Lao, is used in schools, so that children of minority groups have to learn it or be in danger of falling behind in their studies and thus disadvantaged in society. Lao is becoming essential in a modernising society.

Sending Picture Books to Laos

Anxious about this situation, ASPB, later Deknoylao, started its activities, firstly by sending English and Japanese picture books to Laos. Although Lao children could not understand these languages, they could enjoy the pictures and stories, since the pictures tell the stories eloquently. However, as children came to want to understand the plots completely, our NGO started preparing Lao translations of these books. As a result, we currently have 97 titles which have been translated into Lao. Among these picture books, 70 titles are of Japanese origin, the remaining 27 being books translated into Japanese from English. These 97 books were selected for their enduring popularity around the world, since ASPB judged that books which had been loved by children in many countries for a long time would be loved by Lao children as well. After picture books with Japanese text have been collected, Lao translations are glued on to the pages, and they are sent to Laos. Many volunteers have been engaged in this activity in Japan: student clubs, school libraries, and business people. In 2003, with the help of many volunteers, 1,078 picture books were sent to Laos.

The process involves firstly the collection of picture books which are listed as having Lao translations. The list includes classics such as *Where the Wild Things Are* by Maurice Sendak; *Harry the Dirty Dog* by Gene Zion; *The Very Hungry Caterpillar* by Eric Carle; and *Millions of Cats* by Wanda Gag.[2] The Lao translations are by people, such as the representative of the NGO, who have experience of translating into the Lao language. Checking the Lao version against the Japanese, we insert these translations on each page. If there is enough space, the Japanese text is not covered by the translation, and can be seen by the Lao children studying Japanese. We also send picture books in English without these translations so that they can be used as English textbooks. Additionally we send picture books without text, or ones which children can enjoy without understanding the text, such as illustrated reference and art books.

In the past, the most popular language in Laos was French, because of the colonial history. After Laos became a socialist country, many people began to study Russian, but more recently English has become popular, since knowledge of English enhances employment prospects. English text books, including those used for Teaching English as a Foreign Language (TOEFL) and for the Test of English for International Communication (TOEIC), are available at market book stalls. Furthermore, in Vientiane, the capital of Laos, many English language schools have been opened recently.

Although the provision of children's books in English and Japanese, with or without Lao translations, is useful, the NGO came to regard it as insufficient. It is also necessary to produce children's books in Laos itself. We consider it important to assist local writers, publishers and teachers in the production of 'their own' books. Therefore Deknoylao has embarked on new activities which aim to encourage the production of children's books in Laos.

Producing Children's books in Lao

In 1990, Deknoylao published the first book written in Lao, *The Legend of Planet Surprise.* It is written by Japanese author Shinji Tajima, founder of the International Centre of Literacy and Culture (ICLC) and a specialist in literacy. This book contains five short stories; 'Konkichi,' 'Someone,' 'The Legend of Planet Surprise,' 'The Dinosaur of the Desert,' and 'Where Does the Spring Come From?' Although some of these stories have Japanese settings, the book deals with global problems, such as conflict and illiteracy. This book was 'dedicated to children, and adults as well, who in spite of doubts and difficulties turn with hope and determination to face the approaching 21st century.' So far, this book has been translated into many languages in Asia, and distributed in countries such as Vietnam, Bangladesh, Malaysia, Laos, Thailand, India, Korea, China, Indonesia, Myanmar, Singapore, Pakistan, Sri Lanka, and Mongolia. Picture books in the Lao language have also been produced for literacy education: *What Kind of Animal is it?* (book 1 & 2) and *Twinkling Stars.*

The authors and illustrators of these books are Laotian, but many countries have been involved in producing them. The first editions were printed in Bangkok and Udon Thani, Thailand, but they have been printed in Laos from the second edition onwards, and the quality of printing in Laos is currently improving. The number of printing houses is increasing, and the cost of printing is becoming cheaper.

The books have been funded by charitable donations from the postal savings for the international voluntary aid system of Japan Post, Canon, The Japan International Cooperation Foundation and others. Donors are not only Japanese: our NGO has been collaborating with donors from various countries, including Canada and France. For instance, in 2003 Deknoylao published Perrault's *Little Tom Thumb* in Lao in conjunction with the France Centre in Laos.

The picture books for literacy education were produced at picture book creating seminars, which were held in Laos. Deknoylao sponsored the travel of Japanese picture book authors to Laos for these seminars. Pictures for the books entitled *What kind of animal is it?* were chosen from among those drawn by participants in the seminar, who included authors (most of whom have other jobs, because it is difficult to make a living as an author in Laos), teachers in schools and kindergartens, and government officials. For *Twinkling Stars*, our NGO held a competition that required participants to draw illustrations for selected poetry, after which we selected pictures for each poem. In our office in Laos, children can often be found reading aloud from these books.

We are currently planning to encourage entertainment books, since there are still few comic books or magazines in Laos. One which does exist is *Lao Animal Stories in Pictures*, based on an ancient Indian story *Tantra*, retold by a Lao author. On the other hand, Kamishibai (a story told with pictures) has come to be an important Laotian medium. Because of the rich oral tradition in Laos, Kamishibai, originally a Japanese style of storytelling that involves the audience, was considered to be appropriate to Lao culture. We have sent specialists in Kamishibai to Laos, and held Kamishibai-creating seminars and competitions.

This year, Deknoylao has published its hundredth book in Lao, *Where am I going?* This is written by Japanese authors and illustrators, and translated into Lao by our representative there. It is aimed at environmental education, since the increasing amount of rubbish in cities and streets has become a problem. Foods used to be wrapped in banana leaves which could be thrown away, since they were biodegradable. Unfortunately, people now throw away plastic wrappings as if they were banana leaves. This book describes the difference between banana leaves and plastic, and highlights the environmental problems.

Other activities

Distribution of books is also regarded as an important activity, as such a system has not been developed in Laos. Our NGO started distributing books via 'portable book bags.' We fill these bags with books, and send them to rural areas. Alternatively, teachers go to schools carrying these bags full of books. Thanks to this activity, more than two thousand schools in both in the capital and rural areas have so far received books.

As well as publishing and distribution, maintaining spaces for children is an important activity, and Deknoylao established the Children's Culture Centre (CCC) in Vientiane, the capital of Laos. Although it is used as a library, it is also a place for activities such as drawing or practising traditional dancing.

Challenges

During these activities, Deknoylao had several difficulties:

Firstly, the concept of a 'good' picture book is a difficult issue to deal with between Japan and Laos, because each culture has its own idea of what constitutes quality. What kind of book is suitable for children? What kind of picture is good? What combination of colours is beautiful? As these matters differ from culture to culture, we cannot insist on our own ideas.

Secondly, we cannot publish books freely in Laos because Laos is a socialist country. Although Laos has many ethnic minorities, we cannot publish books in their languages. Therefore, the books which we have been publishing are not for all the children in Laos but only for those who speak Lao. We understand the possibility that by distributing Lao books to elementary schools around the country we might be aiding the assimilation policy of the Lao government. Nevertheless, we consider it vital to publish these children's books in Lao, for it is difficult to participate fully in today's world without a literate culture. Knowing Lao is necessary for all Laotian people fully to participate in society.

Notes

1. UNESCO Institute for Statistics (UIS), Literacy and Non-formal Education Section. Youth (15-24) and Adult (15+) Literacy Rates by Country and by Gender for 2000-2004 (http://www.uis.unesco.org/TEMPLATE/html/Exceltables/education/Literacy_National_July04.xls) 26th Jan. 2005

2. Titles of some of the chosen books are in the Appendix

Appendix

Examples of some of the books provided and translated into Lao:

Sakasama (*Topsy-Turvies, Pictures to Stretch the Imagination*), Mitsumasa Anno

Eleven Hungry Cats, Noboru Baba

The Three Billy Goats Gruff, Marcia Brown

Miffy series, Dick Bruna

The Little House, Virginia Lee Burton

The Very Hungry Caterpillar, Eric Carle

Play with me, Marie Hall Ets

Millions of Cats, Wanda Gag

Little Blue and Little Yellow, Leo Lionni

Guri and Gura, Rieko Nakagawa and Yuriko Omura

Nenaiko Dareda, Keiko Sena

Where the Wild Things Are, Maurice Sendak

The Great Enormous Turnip, Aleksei Tolstoi

Koguma-chan itai itai, Ken Wakayama

Rabbit's Wedding, Garth Williams

Harry the Dirty Dog, Gene Zion

2. Patterns of Development in Children's Literatures Across the World

Gillian Lathey

Consideration of the situation in Laos prompts a wider look at some of the concepts underlying comparative understandings of children's literature throughout the world.

Universal Children's Literature

An idealistic and romantic view of world children's literature permeated the work of European comparatists in the early twentieth century. In his influential treatise *Les Livres, les Enfants et les Hommes,* first published in 1932, Paul Hazard asserted that children's literature was by its very nature universal. He wrote passionately about his vision of a 'world republic of childhood' that would guarantee every child the right to the creativity, imagination and aesthetic qualities inherent in classic children's literature. But Hazard limited his discussion of cultural difference to books by European (largely north European) children's authors, as did many European critics influenced by his work.

Throughout the 1960s and 70s, Austrian Richard Bamberger (1978) endorsed Hazard's faith in the power of literature to promote internationalism. He suggested that since children across the world share the imaginative worlds created by translated children's writers, 'we can now rightly speak of a genuine world literature for children which can do much to further international understanding' (1978: 21). And, of course, the great and indefatigable founder of IBBY, Jella Lepman, put this vision into practice in the post-war period in an attempt to heal the wounds of war through children's books. (For an account of the international children's book exhibition she organised in Munich in 1946 that led to the foundation of the International Youth Library, see Lepman's autobiography *A Bridge of Books*, 2002). Lepman's approach towards world children's literature was, however, far more broadly international than Hazard's or Bamberger's, and led to the distribution by IBBY of children's books to countries across the globe.

Patterns of development in children's literatures

Such idealistic internationalism was instrumental in combating illiteracy, but rested on the translation and dissemination of European and English-language texts. An assumption that all children's literatures develop along the same lines is also indicative of a European perspective on world literature. In *The Poetics of Children's Literature* (1986), Zohar Shavit establishes a universal model based on the examples of British, German and Hebrew children's literature, whereby the earliest children's texts were produced for didactic purposes to teach literacy, knowledge of the world or moral education. She regards the Enlightenment as a turning point in the history of these case study literatures. Children's literature had to develop separately from this point precisely because of its educational function, and because of the need to combat the attractions of popular literature such as the chapbooks of the eighteenth century. Only at a later stage in its evolution was children's literature regarded as entertainment. From this summative description Shavit concludes; 'I contend that the very same stages of development reappear in all children's literatures, regardless of when and where they begin to develop' (1986: 133ff).

Yet Emer O'Sullivan questions the universality of this trajectory from 'instruction to delight' in her comprehensive history of comparative children's literature, *Kinderliterarische Komparatistik* (2000). Her counter-argument rests on two examples, the first of which is the development as recently as the 1980s of an English-language Irish children's literature published in the Republic of Ireland. Irish writers, who had previously been dependent on American and British publishers, began to create a new literature that was free to assert its independence, and certainly did not focus on pedagogical issues.

Secondly, O'Sullivan turns to the role of colonisation in determining the form, content and purpose of children's literature in black Africa, since books brought by missionaries dominated children's reading in Africa for many years. Imported children's literature undoubtedly fulfilled an educative function in the first instance, not least in promoting literacy in the language of the colonisers. But when and how did indigenous children's writers begin to break away from the didactic colonial tradition and produce a new literature that represented both Africa's traditions and contemporary African life? Patterns of development are certainly not uniform. In an unpublished paper, Mabel Komasi reports, for example, on the growth of a Ghanaian children's literature fostered by seminars and workshops organised in the 1970s and 1980s that contributed to the awareness that Ghanaian children needed to read books related to their cultural background (Komasi: 9).

One key factor in Ghana and elsewhere in Africa is the dominance of the colonial languages. Ashcroft, Griffiths and Tiffin examine this aspect of the post-colonial emergence of indigenous literatures in *The Empire Strikes Back* (1989) where they discuss the decision of Kenyan writer for adults, Ngugi wa Thiong'o, to reject the coloniser's language later in his career in favour of Gikuyu or Ki-Swahili (1989: 130). Yukie Ito's example of support for children's books written in the Lao language emerges from a different historical and political context, but it also draws attention to the significance of the language issue alongside a rethinking of content.

The globalisation of children's literature

Finally, the effect of the accelerating global distribution of mass media, comic books and popular literature on indigenous children's literatures has become a dominant factor in the last twenty years. Sheila Ray in her article on 'The Far East' in Peter Hunt's *International Companion Encyclopedia of Children's Literature* (1996) writes of the struggle to produce indigenous children's literature in the face of a flood of imports from the west, particularly in Malaysia and Singapore where the books of Enid Blyton are still very popular: 'Singapore imports so many English and American children's books, with no need for translation, that local publishers see little point in trying to compete' (Ray, 1996: 823). The globalisation of children's films and books, from Mickey Mouse to Harry Potter, has led to the establishment of what Jack Zipes in *Sticks and Stones* (2000) calls 'the culture industry'. Only government-funded projects, for example the Arts Council of Ireland (which gives financial support to children's publishers), internal children's literature lobbies, or external agencies such as the Japanese NGO described by Yukie Ito, can ensure that indigenous children's literatures survive such economic pressures.

Examples from workshop discussion

Yukie Ito's example of the Laotian initiative and the issues raised above led to examples of further diversity in developmental patterns. Two delegates from the Philippines spoke of the effect on children's literature of successive colonial powers – Spanish and American – and the resurgence of the oral tradition in the post-colonial era. The 'thumbnail history' of children's literature in the Philippines by Lina B Diaz de Rivera (2004) also emphasises the role of pre-colonial tribal teachers and storytellers called the *babaylan* who spoke in verse, and whose traditions were exploited in the early years of the Spanish conquest. It was only in the twentieth century, however, that a separate written Philippine children's literature began slowly to come into its own with the stories of Lola Basyang (pseudonym for Severino Reyes) in the 1920s and 30s, and the work of the Children's Communication Center that began in the 1970s (de Rivera).

Another delegate described how, in a radical revision of the 'instruction to delight' model during the Communist era, traditional tales were suppressed in the Ukraine in favour of socialist realism during the early and mid-twentieth century. The heavily didactic nature of such realist texts is yet another twist in the evolution of children's literature that belies any notion of uniformity.

The symbiosis of instruction – whether in a strictly pedagogical or more generally ideological sense – and entertainment is, as these examples suggest, subject to political and economic imperatives that make each children's literature unique. Vested adult interests in the ideological manipulation of children's literature also raise a final question as to the necessity of a separate literature for children: is this divergence from a literature for all, whether oral or written, a 'natural' and inevitable development? Do all indigenous literatures develop in this way? It rapidly became clear to workshop delegates that comparative study of the development of children's literatures beyond Europe and the US is as intriguing as it is neglected, at least by western scholars.

Bibliography

Ashcroft, Bill, Griffiths, G and Tiffin, H (1989, 2nd. edition 2002) *The Empire Writes Back,* London: Routledge

Bamberger, Richard (1978) 'The Influence of Translation on the Development of National Children's Literature', in Klingberg, G and Ørvig, M (eds.) *Children's Books in Translation,* Stockholm: Almqvist and Wiksell, pp19-27

Diaz de Rivera, Lina B (2004) 'Children's Literature in the Philippines: A Thumbnail History', *Diliman Review,* Vol. 51 No. 4, pp5-9

Hazard, Paul (1932) *Les Livres, les Enfants et les Hommes*, Paris: Flammarion

Lepman, Jella (2002) *A Bridge of Children's Books: The Inspiring Autobiography of a Remarkable Woman*, Dublin: O'Brien Press

O'Sullivan, Emer (2000) *Kinderliterarische Komparatistik,* Heidelberg: C Winter

Ray, Sheila (1996) 'The Far East' in Hunt, P (ed.) *International Companion Encyclopedia of Children's Literature,* London: Routledge, pp79-85

Shavit, Zohar (1986) *The Poetics of Children's Literature,* Athens: University of Georgia Press

Zipes, Jack (2000) *Sticks and Stones,* New York: Garland

Part 3

A Celebration of the Work of Diana Wynne Jones

Celebrating the Work of Diana Wynne Jones

Diana Wynne Jones was born in August 1934 in London, where she had a chaotic and unsettled childhood against the background of World War II. The family moved around a lot, finally settling in rural Essex. As children, Diana and her two sisters had little access to books. So, armed with a vivid imagination and an insatiable quest for good books to read, she decided that she would have to write them herself. She has written both children's books and plays, and has published over forty books. *Charmed Life*, the first book in the Chrestomanci series, won the 1977 Guardian Award for Children's Books. In 1999, she won two major fantasy awards: the children's section of the Mythopeic Award in the USA and the Karl Edward Wagner Award in the UK.

The 2004 IBBY Conference provided a good opportunity to celebrate Diana Wynne Jones and her work. The paper in this section by Nikki Humble is a scholarly yet personal discussion of an area very relevant to studies of Jones' work There follow shortened versions of two plenary talks given at the conference, and a synopsis of a workshop paper which cannot be included here in full form because of other publishing obligations.

The Rewards of Intertextuality: The Mythic Dimensions of the Work of Diana Wynne Jones

Nikki Humble

I should begin by saying that I approach Diana Wynne Jones's work as an enormous fan. When I've worked on her books in the past, I've thought about them in the context of their treatment of time, and interest in multiple worlds, but for this paper, I started with something more personal and more immediate: why do I enjoy her work so much? What is it that is so compelling about her fantasies? I thought back to my first encounter with the work: my finding The Homeward Bounders in my school library at the age of sixteen. I had read plenty of fantasy narratives before, but none had gripped me in quite the same way. The book left a haunting residue of images in my mind: of the shadowy figures in their triangular building, playing war games which determine the fate of worlds; of the girl with the withered arm that turns out to be the source of her extraordinary powers; of the homeward bounders journeying endlessly on, caught between worlds; and most of all of Jamie, the protagonist, finally making it back to his own world, only to discover that he is a hundred years too late - and the devastatingly bleak concluding moments in which he reveals that while the other homeward bounders can return to their own worlds, he alone will have to keep travelling endlessly on, always moving, belonging nowhere, in order to keep all the separate linked worlds real. These are mythic notions, and they escape the book in the way that the elements of myth escape the culture that engenders them: they detach themselves from the narrative and continue to resonate, to haunt. Myth is one of the primary engines of Diana Wynne Jones's work - it informs her structures, and weaves itself through her narratives. And it seems to me that myth has much to do with the peculiar power of these books. Of course, a great deal of children's literature engages with myth, but I want to argue that there is a very particular pattern to Jones's employment of the mythic, and that it is intimately connected to her approach to her readers: one that challenges, entices, and consistently speaks up to them.

Myth, and its related modes of legend and folklore, is everywhere in Jones's work: in the Celtic underpinnings of The Power of Three and The Time of the Ghost, in the Arabian Nights tales that feed into Castle in the Air, in the northern European folk traditions of Howl's Moving Castle and Fire and Hemlock. The Ancient Egyptian worship of Sirius underlies Dogsbody, Ancient Greek myths structure The Homeward Bounders and feed into The Ogre Downstairs, and the Norse legends are central to Eight Days of Luke. King Arthur appears in the figure of the sleeping once-and-future-king that literally underpins Time City, and again in the computer-game surrealism of Hexwood, while a strangely familiar, though apparently invented, mythology structures the bitter gender politics of Black Maria. I'm not claiming any prizes for pointing this out - it is a very obvious feature of Jones's work. What

I am interested in pursuing a little further, though, is the way in which she uses these mythic elements.

The first example I would like to consider is *Eight Days of Luke*, first published in 1975. It begins as a realist story of an orphaned boy who lives, when not at boarding school, with his unpleasant aunt, uncle and cousin (sound familiar?). Faced with a lonely, frustrating summer, and angry with his uncaring relations, David stands on the compost heap and utters what he hopes is a powerful curse (again, rather familiar ...). The garden wall falls down, and the enigmatic Luke appears and proceeds to change David's life. From this point on the book works rather like a detective story. Luke's identity is a puzzle, and there are clues peppered throughout the narrative to help us work it out. He is a creature of fire - appearing when a match is struck, and conjuring flames at will. He is mischievous, charming and without conscience. He is scared of the new gardener, Mr Chew. Other characters appear - the new neighbour, Mr Fry; the charismatic Mr Wedding; the strapping ginger-haired young man who catches Luke on a Thursday ... Some clues are made easy for us – 'Funny', David jokes at one point 'that Mr Chew turned up on Chewsday' (1984: 70). Luke, it turns out, has committed a dreadful crime long ago, for which he was locked in an underground prison. Mr Wedding and the others are desperate to recover a precious and mysterious object which Luke had helped someone else to hide. David offers to find the object, the name of which he cannot know, in exchange for Luke's freedom. This is the passage in which he finally succeeds:

> It was not strictly a tomb. It was more a heap of rocks piled up to mark the top of the hill and now holding the statue. David looked down at the statue and, with a jump of horror, found it was a body... The body was wearing queer old armour, not quite like that of a knight of old, but not unlike, and the flames made that look copper too. David guessed that if whoever it was had been alive and standing up, he would have been as tall as Mr Wedding.
>
> Then he looked on to the body's face and found it was a lady... It seemed such a pity that David put out his hand and gently touched the lady's hair, which spread out in long twisted strands from her strange helmet. It might have been brown hair, but the flames made it seem coppery. As he touched it, he knew she was alive. There was a warmth about her that did not come from the fire. So he put his knuckles to her face and gave it a gentle push.
>
> The lady did not move. Wondering why not, David looked at her chest to see if she was breathing. Because of the armour she was wearing, he was quite unable to tell. But there was a very strange object lying across her chest, now he came to look. It looked a bit like a pick-axe

> and seemed to be made of stone - anyway it was made of something the flames did not turn coppery... Everything about it suggested that it was much older than the rest of the lady's equipment.
>
> Luke had said the thing would be the odd thing out. David said 'Of course' and was just about to snatch up the pick-axe triumphantly, when he stopped and thought. It would do no good to come away with the wrong thing. That would be all his trouble for nothing, and Luke dragged off to a worse prison than before. He took the hospital disc out of his pocket to make sure.
>
> Visitor Admit One, it said. David turned it over. The number had vanished from the other side. It now read Firestone and, underneath, HAMMER. (pp165-6)

By now David himself has worked it out:

> David looked uncertainly at the pick-axe again. Yes, the blunt end could be a hammer - it must be a hammer - if the disc said hammer, then it was a hammer and the thing he had been looking for. But the reason for his hesitation had nothing to do with that. Of course it was a hammer, and he knew who the man was who owned it now. The trouble was, he knew who Luke was too, and he would never be able to think of Luke in the same way again. (1984: 167)

The reader, too, has probably got at least part of the way there by now: it comes as little surprise to most, I would imagine, when David hands the hammer to the ginger-haired young man: '"Here you are," he said. "Your name's Thor, isn't it?"' (1984: 169). But the other mythic elements of the puzzle are more obscure. David himself knows some things: 'He remembered now that Luke had been put in prison for killing someone called Baldur' (1984: 172), and Mr Wedding/ Wodin explains that the woman in the flames is Brunhilda, and summarises the history of her doomed relationship with Siegfried. What he doesn't tell us - and the matter on which the text itself remains resolutely silent - is Luke's real name. This is because the text is a riddle - and the one word that cannot be spoken in a riddle is its answer. If you do know the answer, there is a curious satisfaction in supplying it yourself. If you don't, you are haunted by the lack, but have been given enough information to find it out for yourself.

I want now to summarise the myths connected to this elusive character - whose name, of course, is Loki. In Scandinavian mythology, Loki was a trickster figure, a handsome giant possessed of great knowledge and cunning which he used both creatively and with malice. One such incident involved Balder, the god of light and joy, the son of Odin and Frigg, the king and queen of the gods. Having dreamed that Balder's life was threatened, Frigg extracted a promise from all the forces and beings in nature that they would not harm him, but forgot to include mistletoe in the oath. The gods, thinking Balder could not be killed, played a game in which they threw darts and stones at him. Loki put a twig of mistletoe in the hands of Balder's twin, the blind Hoder, god of darkness, and helped him aim at Balder, who died when the dart pierced his heart. In revenge, the gods seized Loki and put him in irons. Loki's crime and punishment were to have a decisive effect on the history of the gods:

> The Teutons did not believe that the world would endure for ever nor even that the gods were immortal. Like men, the gods had ceaselessly to struggle against enemies who were full of envy and deceit... To maintain their pre-eminence over these demons they had incessantly to remain on the alert... But in spite of the precautions taken and in spite of their warlike virtues the Aesir [Norse gods] were to finish by succumbing to their enemies. And the world which they had sustained and protected was to crumble in ruins with them.
>
> To this grandiose catastrophe... the name Götterdämmerung or the 'Twilight of the Gods' has been given...It was the murder of Balder which marked the beginning of the great ordeal. Before his body the Aesir swore an oath to avenge him bitterly. They were not unaware that it was Loki who had armed and guided the hand of the blind murderer. They seized him at once and put him in irons. This ignominious treatment only served further to envenom the wicked god. He broke the chains and joined the Aesir's irreconcilable enemies, the demons and the giants, and with them fought against his former companions. (Larousse, 1961)

What I find interesting is how Jones locates us in time in relation to these myths: Siegfried is dead, and to be found in the heroes' heaven, Vallhalla - represented in the fiction as an amusement arcade. Loki is out of prison, and a thousand years has passed since the heyday of the Norse Gods, while the final battle - Ragnarock - has yet to come. But the *Eddas* - the tenth to thirteenth century Scandinavian records of these stories - are curious in not putting the twilight of the Gods in some eternally unreachable future: their Gods do not live or rule for ever, and the great battle, although it has not yet happened, is known in all its details. Wynne Jones gestures towards these paradoxes in the fact that her Norse Gods seem to know what is to come:

> Mr Wedding sighed... These things have to be, Luke. We've been in a poor way, these last thousand years, without the hammer. Other beliefs have conquered us very easily. But now, thanks to David, we'll have our full strength for the final battle.' He turned and looked at Luke, smiling slightly. Luke looked back and did not smile at all.
>
> It came home to David that Luke and Mr Wedding were going to be on opposite sides, when that final battle came. (1984: 173)

She gives us no more than this. She is careful to keep Luke/Loki as the charming trickster figure of the earlier Norse myths, and to delay his collapse into the near-demonic figure he becomes in the Christianised *Eddas* which tell of Ragnarock. Yet our attention is specifically drawn to that last battle, and Loki's joining with the forces of evil against the other gods: the darkness is extra-textual, only retrievable through a knowledge of the sources, but it is there. Luke is given a little extra time - perhaps the mere eye-blink of a human life-span - in which to be a charming boy, but his future beckons inexorably.

This sense of dark futures, of mythic fates, also strongly informs *The Homeward Bounders*. Journeying endlessly around the bounds and the linked worlds, Jamie meets other homeward bounders, among whom are the ragged mariner sailing ever-onwards on his ghost-like ship, and the mad old tramp who says his name is Ahasuerus. The first is the Flying Dutchman, a haunted figure in nautical legend - a Dutch mariner, accursed for uttering a blasphemous oath in the presence of God, who is doomed to sail eternally about the Cape of Good Hope, his ship boding disaster for any sailors who saw it. The second is the Wandering Jew, a figure who flourished in European legend from the sixteenth to the nineteenth centuries - a Jew who taunted Christ as he bore the cross to Calvary, urging him to go faster, and was for his offence condemned to wander the world eternally. In Jones's text they step out of the pages of myth to reveal themselves as more homeward bounders, whose fate as eternal wanderers has less to do with theological transgressions than with the whim of *Them*, the shadowy game-players who control the universes:

> He sighed. 'You have not heard of me in your world maybe? In many places I am known, always by my ship, always sailing on. The name most often given is that of Flying Dutchman.'
>
> As it happens, I had heard of him. At school - good old boring chapel-shaped Churt House - one rainy afternoon, when all the other Dominies were down with flu. The one Dominie left had told us about the Flying Dutchman, among other stories. But all I could remember about him was that long, long ago he had been doomed to sail on for ever, unless - It didn't matter. It was probably the same as me.
>
> 'What happened? What did you do to annoy *Them*?' I asked.
>
> He shivered, and sort of put me aside with that skeleton hand of his. 'It is not permitted to speak of these things, he said. Then he seemed sorry. 'But you are only young. You will learn.'(1990: 39)

And this is the Wandering Jew:

> 'Listen to me. Listen to the wisdom of Ahasuerus, who was among the first to have the mark of Cain set on him.'
>
> I think that's how he said his name. It sounded like a sneeze. 'Listen to who? I said. 'Ahasuerus,' said the old tramp. 'The same whom they term the Wandering Jew.' ...
>
> '*They* gave me to hope,' Ahasuerus said. '*They* hung me in hope as one in chains, and put a goal before me and set me on my way. But that goal always retreats from me, as mirage in the wilderness or star from star. I am weary now and hope is a heavy burden. And *They* put a lie in my mouth, so that I may not tell the worlds about *Them*, but must say that I sinned against God. But this is a lie, and there is power in numbers. Before three of my own kind, I may speak the truth. For I was born with more sight than most, and I saw *Them*. I saw the gaming-board of *Them* and I saw the game *They* played with the nations. And I went out to preach and warn my people of *Their* coming ploy. And for that reason, *They* took me, Ahasuerus, and hung chains upon me, and sent me forth with lies in my mouth, and I am called the Wandering Jew.' (1990: 143-4)

The sin against the Christian God of the originating mythologies is transformed into a trespass against *Them*. But who are *They*? Another mythic figure in the story gives us a clue. This is the man Jamie finds chained to a rock, with a gaping wound in his side, waiting for the vulture who will attack him once more. Like Loki, he is never named: Jamie calls him simply 'him'. He is, of course, Prometheus. In Greek mythology, Prometheus was a Titan, one of the fathers of the Gods, who was given the task by Zeus of creating humanity. To help his creation, Prometheus stole fire from heaven, for which transgression Zeus had him chained to a rock in the Caucasus, where he was constantly preyed on by an eagle. Wynne Jones's Prometheus gives a rather different explanation for his imprisonment: '*They* put it about on most worlds that I was punished for lighting fires. I think only the world of Uquar knows the truth.' (1990: 208-9). Prometheus had discovered the key facet of the linked multiverses - the way to remove reality from the worlds and locate it outside them - in the space that *They* now use for their game-playing. To maintain this state, the homeward bounders were necessary - individuals who moved between the worlds, while maintaining constantly the hope that they would return to their own Real place one day. Hope, as the Wandering Jew declares, is the thing that paradoxically chains them to their fate: it is only because Jamie loses all hope that he manages to defeat *Them*. And hope, of course, is also the one thing left in the chest of Pandora, Prometheus's fatally-curious sister-in-law. The logic of the linked universes is rather shadowy - it seems to me not as fully worked out as in later fictions, particularly the 'Chrestomanci' sequence. But that is part of the way it achieves its mythic effects. Incidentally, this is why the 'Chrestomanci' stories did not form part of my initial list of stories with a mythic element. In them, science replaces myth as an explanatory force; although they are about magic it is a bracingly realistic, explainable sort of magic. The two traditions are brought together in Wynne Jones's more recent books, notably *A Tale of Time City* and *Hexwood*, where the paradoxes suggested by quantum mechanics and virtual reality allow the mythic and the scientific modes elaborately to entwine. To return to Prometheus - it is he who allows us to name *Them* as the Greek Gods - those beings who Prometheus thought were his friends, but who turned against him. Yet *They* are also demons, who can be attacked with the arsenal of demon-fighting equipment supplied by another of the homeward bounders, who comes from a world informed by Eastern mythologies. And the Wandering Jew and the Flying Dutchman, from the Christian pantheon of legends, are also 'true' in this fictional space. But there is no God in the Christian sense, no higher court of appeal beyond *Them*, though the Wandering Jew does talk about him. There are only those terrible wilful beings of King Lear's rage-filled visions: 'As flies to wanton boys are we to the gods,/They kill us for their sport.' Prometheus, in his friendship for mankind and his suffering, perhaps suggests Christ, but it is notable that his role as scapegoat is taken over by Jamie - a very ordinary human boy. Mankind has to save itself. Diana Wynne Jones strikes me as very unusual in this respect: unlike all those other children's writers who employ mythic structures - think Tolkien, C. S. Lewis, Madeline L'Engle, Philip Pullman - she alone does not require a felt religious dimension to her mythology. She writes humanist mythology.

The final story I want to consider is another in which people are preyed on by extra-human forces: *Fire and Hemlock*. The sources for this work spin fantastically out of control, and I don't propose an exhaustive search of them. Just some of the clear influences and inter-texts include Fraser's *The Golden Bough*, T. S. Eliot's *Four Quartets*, and a score of folk tales and ballads. In this novel, the requirement to read actively is laid not just on the reader but on the protagonist, Polly, who has to find out exactly what story she is in before she can defeat the malign forces ranged against her. To summarise - the book begins with the nineteenth-year old Polly, about to return to her second year at University, looking at her belongings in her bedroom in her grandmother's house. A picture of a fire in a field, with a hemlock plant in the foreground starts her thinking back to a time when she had been fascinated by it. Something snags at her attention, and she realises that she has two sets of memories of the last nine years. The rest of the book traces the hidden set of memories, and then Polly's actions in the present when she realises why she has been forced to forget the past. At the centre of the memories is her relationship with the vague Mr Lynn, or Thomas, as she calls him as she grows older, and with the threatening encounters she has, over the years, with the people from the big house at the end of her street -

the house where she gate-crashed a funeral at nine years old, and first met Thomas Lynn. The plot is too complex to summarise briefly, but Polly finally has all the pieces of the jigsaw when she reads *The Oxford Book of Ballads* and finds the stories of Thomas the Rhymer and Tam Lin:

> On the bus to Middleton the following day, Polly sat clutching the book of ballads. She did not need to read those first two. She had them more or less by heart by then. But she thought about them the whole way.
>
> They were both about young men Laurel had owned, but their fates had been rather different. Thomas the Rhymer was a harpist, and a man of considerable spirit. When Laurel proposed rewarding him for his services by giving him the gift of always speaking the truth, Thomas objected very strongly indeed. He said his tongue was his own. But Laurel went ahead and gave it him. And what an awkward gift, Polly thought, one which could be downright embarrassing if Laurel happened to be annoyed when she gave it him. True Thomas, she called him, and turned him back into the world with his awkward gift after seven years. In the book, the story stopped there. But Polly knew she had read a longer version, perhaps in another book Tom had sent her, which made it clear that Thomas the Rhymer was still Laurel's property even after he got home. Years later she came and fetched him away and he did not come back.
>
> The second Thomas had been taken as a boy, and he had escaped. He was rescued by a splendid girl called Janet, who was forever hitching up her skirts and racing off to battle against the odds. When the time came, Janet had simply hung on to her Tam. Laurel, or whatever she had been called then, was furious.
>
> Polly could only hope she might manage to do what Janet had done, but she was very much afraid it would not be quite like that. Despite the similarities of the names, it was not Tam Lin but Thomas the Rhymer whom Thomas Lynn most resembled. (1987: 306-7)

We have to read the ballads ourselves to have it spelt out who Laurel really is - the Queen of the Fairies (those dark, malevolent fairies from the folk tradition, of course, rather than the skippy gossamer-winged variety of Victorian fantasy). In Jones's version she needs to take a new life every eighty-one years, and her king-consort needs a new life every nine. This is the final fate of the young men she seizes to be her companions.

As with *Eight Days of Luke*, the puzzle element is one of the key aspects of the book's appeal, and in this case Jones very carefully directs the reader to the sources that construct her fantasy and which will enable its secrets to be unravelled. Forced to keep away from Polly, Thomas Lynn sends her parcels of books, all of which are listed for us: they amount to a curriculum of reading from the ages of ten upwards, from *The Wizard of Oz* to *The Golden Bough*, via *The War of the Worlds* and *The Man Who Was Thursday*. Not all of them contain clues to the mystery: they are recommendations to the reader from Jones herself as much as they are from Thomas Lynn to Polly. But many do feed directly in to the puzzle - particularly *The Golden Bough*, from which, on two separate occasions, we get a list of chapter titles - repeated so that we don't miss the significance - which reveal very clearly the workings of those aspects of the myth that do not derive directly from the ballads:

> For quite a while after that, Polly lay around fretfully reading *The Golden Bough* and annoying Granny considerably by insisting on having a proper bookmark so that she would not need to lay the book down on its face. She had to mark her page in some way or she kept losing her place, and she could not find where she had left off in Bristol for days. 'The Hallowe'en Fires', was it, or 'The Magic Spring', or 'The Ritual of Death and Resurrection'? Or was it 'Kings Killed When Their Strength Fails', or 'Kings Killed at the End of a Fixed Term'? It took her ages to discover that she had been in the middle of 'Temporary Kings.' (1987: 210)

Polly wins the contest by reading correctly. She plays the Queen at her own game by working out the rules that govern the exchange of the King's life, and the ways in which the King has broken them. She saves her Thomas by reversing the principles of Janet's rescue of Tam: she rejects him in order to free him. She has to mean this rejection for it to be true - and she does. In a clever move, Wynne Jones defuses the dodgiest aspect of the narrative - the relationship between a girl and a man begun when he was adult and she was ten - by having her heroine denounce her hero for exactly this: for taking her over as a child, for using her. It is true, but it is not the only truth, and the book offers hope that they can still be together after all by another ingenious act of reading. To keep the rules that protect Thomas, they can be together nowhere - yet, as the spinning stone vases in Laurel's garden make clear, Nowhere = Now Here. Nowhere is a place - the Fairy kingdom. And Nowhere is the place Polly has rejected Tom, so if they can't be together there, perhaps they can somewhere. The tortuous logic belongs to the realm of fairy tale - or myth. The beings that inhabit this world, particularly in Wynne Jones's use of them, are absolutely bound by such rules - like the games played by Them and the wager Wodin has with David over Luke. They are powerful, but not all-powerful, and they can be defeated by humans who read the rules carefully, who pay attention to the small-print.

Myth, in Diana Wynne Jones's hands, provides that haunting element that takes you outside the text, that lingers when the reading is finished. It also carries that freight of significance that always belongs to the mythic - that sense of transcendent meanings, of things explained. But if, as I have suggested, this is humanist myth, what are the significances with which it provides us? Unlike the work of religious mythographers, I don't think it boils down to a conflict between good and evil. Luke is not evil - he is mischievous - a sociopath, perhaps, but not a psychopath. Laurel is too petty to be the embodiment of evil - the frisson that the text provides is not so elemental: rather, it is a sense of the uncanny. And *They* are always less than grand - they too are petty, with their game-playing and their arcane rules. Instead, these stories offer us that sense of the uncanny - of something beyond and outside our quotidian experience, and simultaneously undermining it. We are left, as we should be in adolescent fiction, with a sense of the strength of the individual, the possibilities of overcoming obstacles through commitment and integrity. But there is something more - something less comfortable. We are also left with a profound sense of ambivalence - for these figures whose true names are not spoken - Loki, Prometheus, the Queen of the Fairies - are essentially liminal beings, not fully god-like, nor fully human, but caught in some state in between. They are tricksy, deceitful, morally ambivalent - and as such they are powerful emblems for the adolescent condition, for the complicating of the moral vision that comes with the end of childhood.

I would like to return finally to my own first encounter with the worlds of Diana Wynne Jones. I didn't just find that first book in a library, I *read* it there - at least a third of it at one gulp, crouched between the shelves - for the rest I managed to make it to a desk. I was so compelled I was unable to leave until I had finished. When I remember that reading, what I see is the library. And having thought about the effects of her fiction, I think that is entirely appropriate. As well as providing powerful suction to pull her readers into her books, Jones impels them outside the text into the library. Hers is the ultimate in 'scritable' writing, to use Roland Barthes's term: she allows the reader to 'write' the text, to supply the final unifying elements of knowledge, to place the last piece of the jigsaw. She opens up new textual worlds, challenges her reader into more reading - and it is the striking generosity of this move that will keep me reading for as long as she keeps writing.

Bibliography

Primary Texts

Jones, D W (1984; first published 1975) *Eight Days of Luke*, Harmondsworth: Penguin

Jones, D W (1990; first published 1981) *The Homeward Bounders*, London: Mandarin

Jones, D W (1987; first published 1985) *Fire and Hemlock*, London: Methuen

Secondary Texts

Larousse Encyclopedia of Mythology (1984) London: Paul Hamlyn

Conclusion: Responses to the Work of Diana Wynne Jones[1]

Nicholas Tucker, critic, broadcaster and academic at Sussex University, told of how he first encountered Diana during World War Two, when he was four and she was six. Both were members of families staying in 1941 in Lanehead, a vast house on the borders of Lake Coniston that had formerly been occupied by Ruskin's Secretary W G Collingwood. Later on, it had been taken over by the Altounyan family, whose children were the inspiration for Arthur Ransome's famous story *Swallows and Amazons.* Ransome's house was just down the lake, and one evening the famous author visited Lanehead ostensibly to meet the children, without, it would seem, making much impact on them. The families living there during the war had been invited by the Quaker owner of the house as something of a social experiment. Children ate separately from parents, and decisions were arrived at communally. It was not entirely successful; husbands were away during the week and wives missed home and sometimes quarrelled. Diana once spent a few happy hours embellishing with her own crayons some drawings she found upstairs, that turned out to be by Ruskin himself. Other children, allowed to play unsupervised by the lakeside, occasionally pushed each other in to the water or out into the lake itself on a raft. The lake looked dark and dreary during the winter they spent there, and the children's resourcefulness for co-operative and creative self-entertainment bore no comparison with the brave and uncomplaining young characters thronging Ransome's novels.

Tucker wondered how important this whole experience had been to pushing Diana in the direction of becoming a novelist herself. Here, after all, were a group of children living in storyland scenery but behaving in very different ways. Around them was a collection of adults, some of them distinctly odd. One couple, for example, liked to talk in German because they thought this language better suited to spiritual values – not an obviously popular belief at the height of the war. Tucker says:

> When I read Diana's stories now, with their mixture of reality and fantasy, hopes and fears, parental control and that total freedom associated in her case with magic, I wonder if she sometimes remembers that very strange time in our young lives. When ordinary domestic life is suddenly turned on its head in so many different and unexpected ways, a child has to respond with a mixture of acceptance and imagination to try to make sense of what is happening. In her own books, children are often faced by equal challenges. The way they survive and indeed thrive always reminds me of Diana herself as a child, a dark, elfin presence fascinated both by what is going on around her and by her own inner world of fantasy and humour laced by her sharp intelligence.

Charlie Butler, children's author and senior lecturer at the University of the West of England, set his response to the work of Diana Wynne Jones into the format of a television phone-in, choosing the ten top qualities which attract readers. He spoke of the *range* of her work: some forty books in thirty years or so, all different, including fantasy, Science Fiction, non-fiction, satire and farce, written for an audience that has ranged from the very young to adults. He commented too on its re-readability, each new read bringing new pleasures and insights. In particular, to read one of the Chrestomanci books again after reading the 'pre-quel', *The Lives of Christopher Chant,* modifies the understanding of all the characters. Jones's knowledge about the technicalities of *magic* and its varieties is also significant in her work: some of her spells are grand, formal affairs, others are almost casual, and sometimes she keeps readers guessing as to whether any magic has actually taken place at all.

Butler went on to praise Jones's striking ways of moving between worlds, and her brilliance at depicting the fantastic in this world, from *Fire and Hemlock's* artful reticence about where magic ends and ordinary reality begins, to the multiply-split and pleated realities of *Hexwood*. He also enjoys her humour: farcical situations are never created simply for laughs but rather to show new ways of seeing the world. She has created a wide range of not only new worlds but new multiverses, each with its own ecology, its own politics and fashion, its own rules of physics, its own magic. Some of these are linked to our own world through having split off from it at earlier points of history; others are connected in different ways, or (in the case of the Dalemark books) not at all. Some of these worlds are no bigger than a village or small town. The coherence of the parts of the world we see convinces us of the rest, because we trust her to have thought through even those things we are not actually told. Her characterisation too is effective; it gives the impression that whatever she tells us about a person is only a small proportion of what she *could* tell. Diana is always helpful in providing her readers with waymarks, which help us navigate our route through her books. Smells, garments, sayings and behaviour tend to work as symbols which convey something about the persons concerned, without making any of these people merely caricatures. Butler finds too that her novels, while showing respect for everyone, display a particular sympathy with the powerless, those who have decisions imposed upon them by others. In effect this often means that she is on the side of children. He finished with praise for both her influence on other children's writers and her personal generosity.

Farah Mendlesohn, lecturer, editor of *Foundation: the International Review of Science Fiction*, and author of a monograph on Diana Wynne Jones, spoke about the way that Jones's fantasy throws the reader's own world into a new perspective. Mendlesohn terms this form of fantasy, set in a world with which the protagonists are intimately familiar and in which their expressions of surprise have to be consistent with what they can be expected to know, *immersive*.[2] She cited as an example *Howl's Moving Castle*:

> When Sophie meets Calcifer for the first time the description happens in her own head, in the context of her own thoughts and imaginings. It is not a description for us, but an attempt to make sense in her own mind of the space around her. She stares into the fire, thinking that she is imagining a fire demon, who then appears, so that there is just a chance that her speculation forced Calcifer into the open. But the real issue is that Sophie is not an outsider in this fantasyland. Indigenous to it, she is in dialogue with the world around her and it is in this dialogue with the fantastic that Jones constructs the immersion. Sophie may be surprised to meet Calcifer, but she is not surprised to meet *something like him*. Jones has written the kind of meeting that takes place in a cocktail party. Too often, this kind of meeting in fantasyland would include a statement which, if transferred into the real world would be the equivalent of remarking to one of one's own species: 'My, you're a *human*.'

Mendlesohn suggested that in her *Dalemark* sequence Jones is successful in destabilising the relationship between past and present. The convention that otherworld fantasy be set in a world somehow similar to our own pasts is followed in all of her Dalemark books except *The Crown of Dalemark*, in which Dalemark is moving through different stages – some places are still agrarian, some in process of industrialising, and some in an artisan culture. Thus the characters themselves need to interpret scenes in terms that fit what they know.

She suggests that Jones also has something to say about how thoroughly or otherwise anyone can be absorbed into a culture not their own. The convention in much fantasy that the protagonist can take on the clothing of another culture and become part of that culture, is challenged for instance in *Drowned Ammet* where, by dressing as a palace boy, a character is suddenly confronted by the physical consequences of poverty.

The result of this destabilising is that the present becomes a rather complex place. A disorienting aspect of this sequence is that Jones has built the world's history and prehistory and then distilled it out, leaving us with only the trace elements that its inhabitants might know. In *Cart and Cwidder*, the first of the novels, Clennan the singer tells his children the legends of Osfameron and the Adon, but because they've heard them before, they are not filtered through to us. In *The Spellcoats* we slowly realise that we are in the pre-history of the Dalemark we met in *Cart and Cwidder*, but then we discover that perhaps this is the root of some of the legends, that the people we are meeting will go on to be gods. Part way through we discover that the first coat is an unreliable narrative, and that it forms the history on which the second coat comments – and this is communicated in part through a shift in tenses. Eventually we learn that this 'historical' place has both a pre-history and a future. What we have been reading is not 'the past' but 'history' mediated both by the coats themselves and the process and context of translation - a remarkably powerful point to make in a novel intended for young teens. The final novel, *The Crown of Dalemark,* selects its protagonist from the future of characters previously met, so that the reader asks which element of this tale is in 'the present.' Is this a science fiction story set in the present with a vision of the future appended? Or is it a time-travel historical in which the protagonist's world is the present?

Jones' story, 'The True State of Affairs' was written long before the Dalemark books, but nevertheless belongs with them. A young woman, Emily, has stumbled from what might or might not be our world into a Dalemark that is in the middle of a war. She constructs her world rather than having it carefully explained by a guide. She is forced to piece the world together through glimpses both physical and linguistic. Emily's descriptions emphasise the constricted (and constructed) view of the stranger, relying on glimpses to build the pattern of the world. Her narrative is itself a translation, characterised by the inevitable difficulties resulting from different concepts held by different cultures; Mendlesohn writes:

> By the end of this story, as elsewhere in her writing, Jones has demonstrated that the past is not a picture window but a truly foreign country. She writes it through the continual juxtaposition of the familiar and the foreign, forcing the reader to translate and then manipulating our misprision in order to estrange us.

Notes

1. The material in this section is derived from summaries provided by the speakers themselves. Slightly fuller versions can be found in the spring 2005 issue of *IBBYLink.*

2. 'Towards a Taxonomy of Fantasy,' *Journal of the Fantastic in the Arts*, 13.2 (2002), pp173-87.

Biographical Notes on Contributors

Marian Allsobrook completed doctoral research at Cardiff University, examining narrative structures in writers better known for their adult texts than for their work for children. She is a member of the International Society for Research in Children's Literature and a contributor to the Routledge International Encyclopedia of Children's Literature. Having taught at secondary level and in higher education, her research interests now are in the authors who bring the wealth of another culture to their work in English, especially to their writing for young people.

Mary Cadogan is a well-known writer, critic, and broadcaster. She is also editor of *Collector's Digest*, a monthly magazine about children's books and story-papers, co-editor of the Just William Society Magazine and has been consultant and contributor to *Twentieth Century Children's Writers*. Her books include *Frank Richards: The Chap Behind the Chums, Richmal Crompton: The Woman Behind William, and Chin Up, Chest Out Jemima*. She has also co-authored three well received books with Patricia Craig, the best known of which is *You're a Brick, Angela! A New Look at Girls' Fiction*. She is a governor of an international school in Hampshire and for over thirty years was the Company Secretary of the Krisnamurti Foundation, an educational trust.

Nicki Humble is a Senior Lecturer in English at Roehampton University. She specialises in nineteenth- and twentieth-century literature with special interests in women's writing, middlebrow fiction, adolescent literature, historiography, and the literature of food. She is the author of *The Feminine Middlebrow Nove1 1920s to 1950s* (OUP, 2001) and the co-author (with Kim Reynolds) of *Victorian Heroines* (Harvester, 1993). She produced the first-ever scholarly edition of *Mrs Beeton's Household Management* for Oxford World's Classics (2000). She broadcasts regularly on subjects including food, women's writing and children's literature. Her cultural history of cookery, *Culinary Pleasures*, will be published by Faber & Faber in 2005.

Yukie Ito studied Education and Children's Literature in Japan, and is currently studying at the MA program in Children's Literature at Roehampton University. She is a member of the Deknoylao (Action with Lao Children) and the International Center for Literacy and Culture (ICLC).

Ann Lazim is Librarian at the Centre for Literacy in Primary Education. She is Chair of the British Section of IBBY and has recently been elected to the Executive Committee of the organisation at an international level. Ann is a part-time student on the MA in Children's Literature at Roehampton and is currently researching and writing her dissertation on the representation of Arabs in children's books.

Gillian Lathey has reached her current post in the National Centre for Research in Children's Literature via a career in infant school teaching and teacher training. Her research interests are the translation and cross-cultural travels of children's books and the work of German-Jewish children's writers and illustrators exiled to the UK during the Third Reich; she has published chapters and articles on this subject and a comparative study of British and German autobiographical children's books set in the Third Reich and the Second World War, *The Impossible Legacy*. She also administers the Marsh Award for Children's Literature in Translation.

Preetha Leela is a children's literature enthusiast. Her fascination with the influence of early twentieth century British children's writing on Indian contemporary writers led to ongoing research on the subject. She holds an MA in Creative Writing from Sheffield Hallam University and is currently teaching English at a Further Education College in London.

Sophie Mackay works as a primary education officer at a Global Education centre in Tower Hamlets in East London, supporting local schools in their teaching about the interconnectedness of countries, cultures and communities across the world. Sophie also works as a visiting lecturer and part-time researcher at the National Centre for Research in Children's Literature at Roehampton University. In 2000 she completed an MA in Children's Literature. Her dissertation focused on the subject of migration in post-colonial fiction for adolescents.

Pat Pinsent has lectured in English at Roehampton University since 1967, during which period her specialism has changed from seventeenth century poetry to Children's Literature. Currently she is mostly involved in supervising the research of MA, MPhil and PhD students, and tutoring students on the MA Distance Learning mode, for which she wrote the material. Her publications include *Children's Literature and the Politics of Equality* and a number of edited books, including the proceedings of the 2003 IBBY conference, *Books and Boundaries*, together with a number of shorter pieces in other publications. She also edits *IBBYLink*, the journal of the British section of the International Board on Books for Young People.

Sandra Williams has recently returned from Singapore where she lectured at the National Institute of Education. She is now Senior Lecturer in English in the School of Education, University of Brighton. Her PhD thesis explored cultural indicators of Englishness embedded in children's literature texts. Currently interested in emergent literature, her recent research has included compiling a bibliography of Singapore children's literature and investigating Nepali identity in *Adventures of a Nepali Frog* by Kanak Mani Dixit.